"Could be just the wakeup call n ~~~~~~~~~~~~~~~~~ nel recognizes how to remain profita~~~~~~~~~~~~~~~~ the industry."

GEORGE D. E. YEZBAK, VP Materials Management, Thos. Somerville Co.

"I thoroughly enjoyed reading a pre-publication volume of *Disruption in the Channel*. With 30 years of hands-on international business development experience under my belt, I could relate very well to the significant issues with which the book deals. Far from taking a Chicken Little approach to the pending falling sky, Steve Griffith and Scott Benfield deal with the topic scientifically and with a wide, far reaching survey of people in the business and apply their own business experience to the model. While most businesses seem to be sticking their collective heads in the sand and hoping for the best—avoiding the inevitable—this publication addresses and deals with real issues which will affect virtually all businesses in the coming years, regardless of industry or focus. This book is a must read for business people— domestic and foreign focused—for product management professionals up to senior level executives with policy making authority. Old school supply chain models are losing their validity at an exponential rate. Manufacturers and distributors beware…"

DEAN McCASKILL, Corporate Development Officer, Turck GmbH, Former Division President, Honeywell International

"Every time I make a retail purchase and see 'made in China' on the box, I wonder when Far East imports will impact the distribution industry. This book helps advise purchasers on the challenges that will shortly impact all distribution … how to manage multiple month lead times; impact on cash flow; warehouse space management; dealing with fluctuating currencies, etc. By the end of this book, I realized the need to prepare now for the inevitable."

MARK WILSON, Director of Purchasing, Swish Maintenance Limited

"The authors' insight and recommendations are also directly applicable to my daily challenges in service delivery. This book is a recommended read for every manager and professional."

TOM BARGSLEY, CPA, Consultant, Jefferson Wells

ABOUT THE AUTHORS

Scott Benfield is president of Benfield Consulting in Naperville, Illinois. He offers marketing, sales, operations, and strategy consulting for distributors and industrial manufacturers. He has worked in a variety of managerial and executive positions for Fortune-rated manufacturers and nationally ranked distributors for two decades prior to establishing his consultancy. He is the author of five books, numerous research projects, white papers, and professional articles. He has a B.A. and M.B.A. from Wake Forest University. He can be reached at (630)-428-9311 or at bnfldgp@aol.com.

Stephen D. Griffith is president of Merrimont Group, LLC, in Troy, Ohio. He offers strategy, general management, and organizational change consulting for manufacturers and distributors in industrial channels. He has worked in executive and managerial positions for Fortune-rated manufacturers and leading manufacturing entities for three decades prior to establishing his consultancy. He is the author of *Disruption in the Channel*, numerous articles, white papers, and research for industrial channels. In addition to consulting, Mr. Griffith is pursuing a Doctorate in Organizational Leadership from Indiana Wesleyan University, where he also teaches graduate courses in statistics, economics, strategy, international business, technology, and operations. He has a B.S. in engineering from Purdue University and an M.B.A. from the University of South Dakota. He can be reached at (937) 573-9376 or sgriffith2353@mac.com.

DISRUPTION
IN THE
CHANNEL

DISRUPTION IN THE CHANNEL

The New Realities of Distribution and Manufacturing in a Global Economy

SCOTT BENFIELD
STEPHEN D. GRIFFITH

POWER PUBLISHING
Incorporated

Indianapolis, Indiana

DISRUPTION IN THE CHANNEL

ISBN-13: 978-0-9787268-3-6
ISBN-10: 0-9787268-3-9

Library of Congress Control Number: 2007941825

This book is manufactured in the United States of America.

Published by Power Publishing
5641 W. 73rd Street
Indianapolis, IN 46278
(317) 347-1051
www.powerpublishinginc.com

Editor: Stephanie Korney
Cover Design: Parada Design

We the authors believe the research methodology, interviews and conclusions to be an accurate picture of current events in North American durable goods channels. The recommendations for analysis and action are based on the research and the authors' considerable experience in durable goods markets. And, as such, the authors believe that diligent reading and practice using the text will result in improved performance. However, the authors have no control over changes in the marketplace, management ability and implementation, and the reactions of suppliers and competitors. Therefore, we respectfully disclaim the results garnered from using the research and conclusions in this text.

Reading the Text

This text was written after the research was conducted in 2007. After the research, we quickly realized that the entire durable goods channel was in for significant change and, instead of simply describing the research, we conducted over 100 hours of interviews with manufacturers, distributors, and other service providers before creating this text. To have a full appreciation of the rather massive changes from off-brands, we suggest reading straight through the text. Even chapters that pertain to distributors should be read by manufacturers and vice versa. By doing this, the reader gets full benefit of understanding the impact of off-brands and how to work within existing channel relationships to maximize gain or diminish loss. However, we realize that managers are under time constraints and, to point readers to subjects of interest, we offer the subject guide below.

– For an overview of the changes wrought by off-brands for different channel members, read the Introduction.

– For an understanding of the survey demographics and the power of off-brands on distributor finances, read Chapter 2.

– For the price advantage, service quality, and availability of off-brands, read Chapter 3.

– To understand how industrial channels can source off-brands including direct relationships and other channel service providers, read Chapter 4.

– To understand which domestic manufacturer channel supports are needed and which aren't and how off-brand services compare to domestic brands, read Chapter 5.

– To understand why domestic brands are declining and what manufacturers should consider, read Chapter 6.

– For distributor management of private label strategies, decline in traditional branding activities and the rise of channel brands supplanting manufacturer brands, read Chapter 7.

– For a strategic understanding of the migration of channel power away from domestic manufacturing to distributors and end users and the decrease in channel costs, read Chapter 8.

– For the significant changes to the distributors' environment from off-brands and the global economy, read Chapter 9.

– For domestic manufacturer recovery strategies and what to do about off-brands, read Chapter 10.

– To lead organizationwide change in adapting to the "Disrupted Channel," read Chapter 11.

– For assurance that this survey is statistically valid and applies to members of the durable goods channel, read Chapter 12.

To create a sense of urgency in your organization about the "Disruptive Changes" due to global manufacturing and off-brands, buy several copies, give them to your key employees, keep a copy by your nightstand, and read and study the whole book.

DISRUPTION IN THE CHANNEL

CONTENTS

CHAPTER one

Introduction

In the late summer of 2006, at a technology conference in Colorado, Rich Vurva, the editor of *Progressive Distributor Magazine*, and Scott Benfield sat down and planned this research project. The two of us had come to believe that the influx of off-brands was beginning to reach a tipping point or, more plainly, it was at a level where members of durable goods channels would begin to take notice, and substantial change was imminent.

We launched the online research instrument in early 2007 and gathered responses through the second calendar quarter. We were unsure if distributors knew what we meant by off-brands. In our parlance, off-brands are goods produced in foreign countries, which carry features and functionality similar to recognized North American brands. Off-brands, as the name implies, are made by lesser-known manufacturers and have found a foothold in North American markets. Typically, they have better price points than domestic brands. Quality is acceptable and, in some instances, superior to established brands. To our surprise, distributors were very familiar with the concept of off-brands. We received a substantial and quick response to our survey and, from initial analyses, had an insignificant amount of respondents who quit the survey, which implies comfort with the questions.

During the survey phase, we were able to bring Steve Griffith in on the project, and his work is crucial in several areas. Steve is currently pursuing a doctorate degree in organizational leadership at Indiana Wesleyan University where he serves as a graduate faculty member teaching business statistics and operations. Steve and Scott had worked together in the early '90s in the industrial marketing function of a Fortune 100 company. Steve has a significant amount of experience in running manufacturing companies that market through distribution, and his perspective greatly improved the final product. He has also built plants overseas and knows full well the power of foreign manufacturing and getting cost out.

Over the years and in our work, we had related stories of wholesale clients who had established connections with off-brands from China, the Pacific Rim, India, and Eastern Europe. They covered industries as diverse as dry cleaning, electrical, plumbing, safety, flooring, and chemicals distribution. The clients agreed about their working relationship with off-brand vendors, stating:

- Off-brands offered a significant price advantage over domestic brands even when domestic brands were manufactured on foreign shores.
- The quality of off-brands was equal to and sometimes better than domestic brands.
- Off-brand manufacturers' support services were catching up to those of domestic brands.
- Off-brands were here to stay, and the industry would slowly but surely move toward purchasing these products.
- Domestic brands that didn't acknowledge off-brands were in trouble, and many would lose significant business if they didn't change.

In our careers totaling some 50 years in industrial markets, we had, many times, experienced the market-altering power of low-cost but high-quality products from foreign shores. Since the late 1990s, the stories of distributors seeking out off-brands have become increasingly commonplace. Therefore, off-brands and their effects on mature channels was no surprise to us or others with a long history in North American industrial markets. As manufacturing moved to Mexico in the early 1990s (NAFTA Accord) and later to China and the Pacific Rim, the companies that were often licensed to manufacture these goods developed a familiarity with domestic markets and eventually sold under their proprietary name(s). As North America is one of the largest markets in the world for durable goods, it was only a matter of time before these companies began selling their goods in our markets and challenging established brands. In Benfield Consulting's earlier research on the effect of North American manufacturing's movement offshore, distributor executives rightly predicted that foreign goods would, over the years, begin to crowd North American markets.[1] Five years ago, sixty percent of distributor executives agreed that foreign-made products would be more prominent in the future and would offer economic incentive for purchase.

The global rise in off-brands is caused by a confluence of events, including the use of the Internet to check price on commodity products, the usage of e-commerce and EDI by distributors to interact with vendors, and the experience of foreign vendors with North American markets while they act as contract or licensed manufacturers. Combine the technologies and events with industrial channels where distributors are growing and consolidating in a razor-thin operating profit environment, and the stage is set for significant changes in the established channels. How much change do we expect in the channel relationships? To educate the reader about expected changes, we offer the next section as a starting point.

Disruption Earned and Learned

The title of this research includes the word "disruption" for good reason. We believe the coming tide of off-brands will have significant change effects on all parts of the traditional channels. It is simply not enough to recognize that off-brands have better price points, comparable quality, and can be private labeled. These changes, while substantial and predictable, are only the tip of the iceberg. There will be, we predict, substantial changes in most distribution and domestic brand companies in the coming years. What changes you ask? Well, consider some of our observations from the research:

- The distribution purchasing function will change significantly. Purchasing managers will learn to deal with exchange rates, foreign agents, container loads, drayage, and central distribution.

- Distributors will need to develop central distribution centers (CDC) or risk being left out of the game.

- Master distributors who source globally will rise in prominence, and some will displace domestic brands. Other channel entrants will emerge to offer distributors the services of domestic brands at significantly lower price points.

- Smaller distributors will be left out of the picture unless they can form alliances, engage the services of sophisticated logistics firms that can consolidate and then deconsolidate sea and air shipments, work with master distributors, or convince cooperatives to get into the game. While smaller distributors participate in off-brand purchases, their ability to buy volume and at full container prices can place them in a non-competitive position unless they can use creative methods to buy at substantially the same terms as their larger competitors.

- Cooperatives, which have significant relationships with domestic vendors, will be placed in an uncomfortable situation and, perhaps, dysfunctional relationships with key vendors.

- Vendor planning and "marketing funds" for sales promotion will slow, and monies will evaporate from domestic brands that lose significant share.

- Distributors will need to learn to exist off decreased sales and margin dollars as off-brand price points are 30% to 40% less than domestic brands.

- Manufacturers with absorption costing mentality and that have relied on marketing events and sales promotion to maintain share will be forced to carefully plan their future moves. It is very difficult to add a lot of marketing value in terms of cooperative funds, industry events, and distributor partnering when products are mature, and the competition is 30% to 40% less.

- Domestic manufacturing, led by executives who earn up to 400% more than the average factory hand and engineers who cost 40% to 80% more than those on foreign shores, will be forced to trim down the executive suite and will likely move their product development to foreign shores.

- Domestic brands may seek relationships with off-brands that will supplant many of their mature products and add value in their ability to secure domestic markets.

- Powerful domestic brands may find that they are losing power in the distributor relationship because consolidating distributors can source from any number of global manufacturing entities.

- Manufacturer "go to market" strategies will be driven to products and channels where they can clearly add value. Sales promotion, special pricing arrangements, and other events will not be enough of an advantage to preserve share. Information on pricing and availability and product specifications are ubiquitous and instantaneous. There are few places for an inefficient producer to hide.

This list is not comprehensive, and we will review the responses that led to these "change events" that are largely underestimated.

Of all the changes that can occur, the ones that distributors tend to fear most are the loss of sales and margin dollars from the purchases of off-brands. Off-brands cost some 30% to 40% less than domestic brands, and distributors worry about what will happen to the operating structure if margin dollars go down a corresponding amount. For example, think of a distributor that sells $80 million of durable goods at a 25% gross margin and an operating income of $2 million. This means that cost of goods sold is $60 million, and operating expenses are $18 million. If the aggregate purchase price on the $60 million cost of goods goes down 30%, then the firm would have $18 million less in material costs on which to price and would risk losing 25% or 4.5 million margin dollars from the $20 million that is typically generated. Add to this the reduction in volume-rebate dollars from lower purchases, and the numbers can be gloomy indeed.

The preceding math, while potentially worrisome, will not be a precipitous event. Off-brands will gain in popularity, but will not, on the whole, be imported in such volumes as to cause an overnight cost of goods decrease of 30% or more. Secondly, many domestic manufactured goods will rise in cost over time and offset the price decrease of off-brands. We are convinced, however, that the influx of off-brands will require navigating with less margin dollars, and distributors who want to maintain a going concern should be mindful of the following:

- Operating costs will need to be scrutinized carefully and budgeted closely for ongoing profitability.
- Service costs will need to be understood. Service capacity as used by customers and/or customer groups can vary significantly depending on their usage of off-brands.
- The sales force, the most expensive part of the marketing mix, will need to be carefully used as operating profit dollars decline.

There are Chicken Little theorists who, because of the falling margin dollars, advise distributors to "stay away" from off-brands. Financially, as we will illustrate, this is not possible. Distributors cannot afford to **not** engage off-brands. In addition, we would argue, off-brands follow an established pattern in market economies where mature products and mature channels become more efficient. We illustrate this in the next section.

Cowboy Economics and Decreasing Costs in Channels

In a recent white paper, we traced the evolution of livestock supply channels from the 1860s through the 1950s.[2] From the historical research, we found the following happening over the nearly nine decades of the livestock supply channel:

- Channels become more efficient and reduce waste at significant pace. The cost of getting livestock to market decreased around 90% during the period.[3]
- Numerous technologies increased the efficiency of the livestock supply chain, including barbed wire, railroads, refrigerated rail cars, telegraph, telephone, refrigerated trucks, and automated silage.
- These technologies were difficult to predict and happened at different times in different parts of the channel.
- The change in channels spawned new industries and destroyed others. Among the deceased are cowboys, ranchers, slaughterhouses in Chicago and Cincinnati, barbed wire manufacturers, etc. Among the winners are drivers of refrigerated trucks, livestock packaging companies, grain fed beef farmers, supermarkets and the consumer.

The lessons from the livestock channels, we believe, are applicable to durable goods channels. Channels do become significantly more efficient over time, and the benefit to the North American economy is that consumers can buy more with less. How much more you ask? Well, taking a market basket of livestock foodstuffs, from 1919 to 2000, the hours of work required to buy the basket fell 80% during the period from 10 to 2 hours.[4] The same economics have applied to durable goods channels since their inception a century ago. However, since the late 1980s, many durable goods distributors have had limited increases in productivity. In 2002 and again in 2004, we chronicled the low productivity of durable goods wholesalers. Using a number of measures, including sales per employee, margin dollars per employee, and Total Factor Productivity, we found that for many distributors productivity had increased nominally more than inflation.[5] And, in a similar study done in 2006, seventy percent of the wholesaler productivity increase from 2001-2005 was from four industries, including computer hardware, motor vehicles and parts, electronics, and pharmaceuticals. Fourteen of the remaining vertical wholesale industries showed small or negative productivity growth over the period.[6]

The upshot of the productivity issue is that, as cost of goods decline, distributors will need to get productivity increases from better use of operating expenses or pretax margins are likely to fall. In the last several years, the base price of many natural resource commodities has risen substantially as China, India, and Eastern Europe grew their economies. This has given distributors increases in profits as the commodity prices grew faster than the cost of inputs including labor and IT. We expect the commodity increases to slow down and the tide of off-brands to increase, which will put a squeeze on profits. Also, contributing to the distributor's recent profit increase is the dampening of wage increases caused by the global supply of low-cost labor. As this supply slows, the domestic wage rate will feel pressure. Approximately two-thirds of distribution's operating expense is in labor costs. Hence, prudent distributors will strive to improve the use of their operating expenses and lower their overall cost to serve. We expect the outsourcing of payables, payroll, and even logistics to help with the productivity issue in distribution. We also expect larger distributors to get better, more educated knowledge workers in functional processes and take cost out. In the end, we believe that with increases in off-brands, low productivity, and the possibility of commodity decreases and labor increases, much of durable goods distribution is set for a significant change event.

Definitions and Caveats

This research is concerned with durable goods[7] channels including traditional channel members of manufacturers, distributors, and associated parties of cooperatives and independent representatives. Durable goods are defined by the U.S. government as products having a life of three years or more. We broaden the definition slightly by including distributed vertical channels that, more or less, are comprised of durable goods, but also have disposables including paper, chemicals, electronics, etc. For calendar 2006, durable goods distribution totaled approximately $2.3 trillion of the approximately $13.2 trillion USGDP. There are approximately 200,000 companies in durable goods distribution across the U.S. The vast majority of these companies have annual sales amounts under $25 million. It has been estimated that approximately 7% or less of these companies are above the $25 million threshold. However, for many industries, most vertical industry purchase volume comes from larger companies.

Similarly, the manufacturing base that supplies durable goods industry is weighted by Fortune-rated firms, but includes many smaller suppliers also. It is not unusual for a vertical industry to have hundreds, and sometimes thousands, of vendors selling through the distribution base. The manufacturer sales, through durable goods distribution and as counted in our survey, totaled approximately $1.7 trillion for 2006. Since many of the manufactured goods sold through North American distribution are domestic brands but are manufactured on foreign shores, the assumption is that these items are competitive with off-brands. The research, however, finds that this is not a valid assumption, and the average purchase advantage of buying off-brands is over 30% less than the domestic brand price. In our survey, we defined off-brands as those goods that did not have a recognized brand name and that did not originate in North America. We also added that the products were likely to be foreign-manufactured and could be purchased directly from the vendor, through a master distributor, through a cooperative, through importers, or through a foreign entity that is financially supported by a domestic vendor. We also excluded counterfeit goods from the survey, but in truth, it is not always *prima facie* evidence for distributors to know if goods are counterfeit. The violation of patent- and brand-protected products is a real concern. In 2006, approximately $155 million in counterfeit goods were seized by U.S. customs, with 90% of these goods coming from China and the Far East.[8] As such, the survey was not designed to include counterfeit purchases by distributors, and we are confident that, for the most part, these purchases were not included in the responses.

In summary, the movement of off-brands to North America is an event that will reshape durable goods channels in the coming years. Many of these changes have already begun, but it is early enough in the cycle to study the trends and act upon them, as well as prepare for events that have yet to transpire. Our wish as authors is that you critically read the research, judge it independently, and act accordingly. The value of the research is in the individual manager's willingness to mix it with his or her unique experience and proprietary research and come to a better understanding of the disruption to durable goods channels caused by globalization.

Scott Benfield, Benfield Consulting
Steve Griffith, Merrimont Group LLC

December 2007

———————

[1] Benfield, Vurva, 2003, *The China Syndrome*, Progressive Distributor Publishing, p. 24.

[2] Benfield, Griffith, 2007, *Cowboy Economics and the Durable Goods Supply Chain,* White Paper at benfieldconsulting.com.

[3] Cox W., Alm R., 1997, *Myths of Rich and Poor*, Basic Books, page 43. (As measured by "hours" of labor for beef and chicken).

[4] Cox W, Alm R., 1997, *Myths of Rich and Poor*, Basic Books, page 41, figure 2.1.

[5] Benfield, S., Vurva, R., 2006, *Restructuring the Distribution Sales Effort*, Brown Books, pp. 6-8.

[6] Fein, A., August 2006, "Where Productivity is Growing in Wholesale Distribution," pp. 2-3, IBM Small Business at ibm.com.

[7] Statistics for Durable Goods Distribution and Manufacturing are taken from U.S. Census and U.S. Government forecasts by NAICS and SIC codes.

[8] Jusko, J., May 2007, *Supply Chain Management: Foiling Fakes,* Industry Week, p. 2.

CHAPTER two

Survey Instrument and Respondent Demographics

The survey instrument was developed for distributors in durable goods markets. It contained questions using both multiple choice and Likert scales, the familiar three-, four-, or five-point scales commonly used in satisfaction surveys where the responses range from "very unsatisfied" to "very satisfied" or "strongly disagree" to "strongly agree." The survey introduced the concept of off-brands in the introductory paragraph and distinguished between these brands and domestic brands made domestically or manufactured overseas. The introductory paragraph also asked that respondents not answer the survey with counterfeit brands in mind. We were and continue to be interested in legitimate off-brands.

The survey instrument contained 33 questions and the sections included were:

- Demographics
- Current purchase practices of off-brands
- Reasons for sourcing off-brands
- Comparisons of channel services between off-brands and domestic brands
- Future purchasing trends of off-brands

- General questions on channel relationships and changes in established channel intermediaries

Confidentiality of respondents was guaranteed and each respondent received a free Executive Summary of the research.

Survey Demographics

Each respondent was asked demographic questions concerning the industry served, size of firm in annual revenues, functional position of respondent, and geographic region. The survey instrument was launched online through the Progressive Distributor website in the first quarter of 2007. In all, we received 170 responses from distributors across North America. The industries served included the following vertical markets:

- Building Materials
- General Line Industrial
- Power Transmission
- Tools and Fasteners
- Hose and Fittings
- Electrical
- Plumbing
- Fluid Power
- Steel
- Gases and Welding
- HVAC and Refrigeration
- Chemicals and Supplies
- Food Service
- Security Hardware

In addition to these 14 identified vertical markets, approximately 15% of responses were from miscellaneous industry verticals serving durable goods markets. While there are close to 50 vertical markets serving durable goods customers, those identified are major markets, and with the approximately

25 additional responses from "Miscellaneous" or unidentified verticals, we are confident that the responses were indicative of the overall purchases of off-brands.

Respondents were from companies that represented the spectrum of revenue ranges.

Figure 2-1 Respondents by Annual Revenue

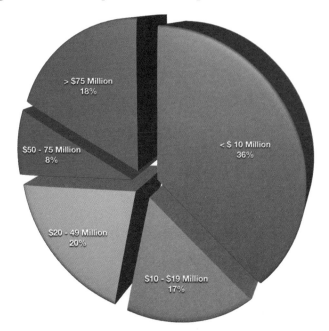

As shown in Figure 2-1, approximately 36.5% of the sample had less than $10 million in sales. Most of durable goods distributors, approximately 75% or more, had less than $10 million in annual revenues. So our sample was weighted toward the larger company. The breakdowns and their exact percentages by revenue range are:

- 36.5% less than $10 million
- 17.1% between $10 million and $19 million
- 20% between $20 million and $49 million
- 8.2% between $50 million and $75 million
- 18.2% above $75 million

Given that close to 50% of the sample had $20 million in sales or more, we are comfortable saying that the respondent base was populated by larger distributors. This skewing of the size ranges is telling in that, we originally believed, the larger distributor has more to gain from off-brand purchases than the smaller firm. The respondent revenue ranges would tend to support our assumptions. We tested the sample responses using t-tests at the 95% level of confidence to see if they were predictive of the population of some 200,000 distribution companies serving durable goods markets. The statistics demonstrated, as shown later in the text and in the Appendix, that we may be 95% confident that these responses are indicative of distributors in general.

The geographic dispersion included firms from all areas of the Continental U.S. and Canada. Figure 2-2 gives the percentage of respondents from geographic areas.

Figure 2-2 Respondents by Geography

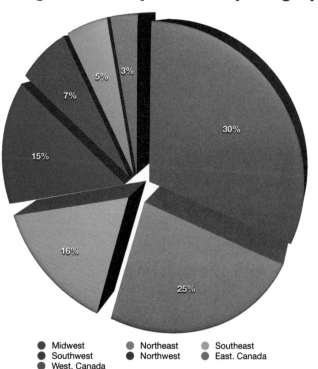

Midwest   Northeast   Southeast
Southwest   Northwest   East. Canada
West. Canada

Approximately 30% of the distributors were from the Midwest and 25% from the Northeast, followed by the Southeast, Southwest and Northwest. Approximately 8% of the responses were from Canadian entities. We can only explain the predominance of responses from the Midwest and Northeast as being due to their population. Both areas of the U.S. have very different industrial bases but they are both populous regions and would be expected to have most of the responses. The Southeast would be a close third in responses, due to its relative population.

Figure 2-3 Respondents by Job Function

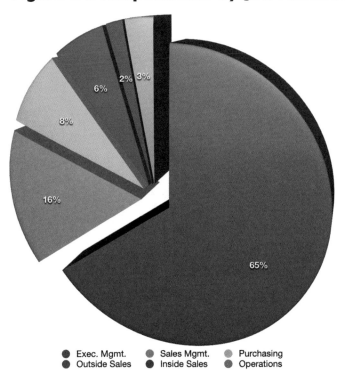

● Exec. Mgmt.   ● Sales Mgmt.   ● Purchasing
● Outside Sales ● Inside Sales   ● Operations

Responses by job function are given in Figure 2-3. The vast majority of the respondents were Executive Management at 65.3%, followed by Sales Management at 15.9%, and Purchasing Management at 8.2% of the sample. The fact that Executive Management has such a predominant number of responses is significant for a number of reasons. First, since the majority of distributors are privately held and managed by family members, executive responses are highly correlated with the strategic direction of the company. Second, the high level of executive respondents versus other functions suggests that distributors view the purchase of off-brands as strategically significant and worthy of their personal investment of time. Executive management can run the gamut in distribution and include various C and V level functions. Most common are President, CEO, COO, CFO, and VP of Materials Management positions. Sales Management and Purchasing Management positions rounded out the top three functions, and again, as sales and purchasing are the more common strategic functions in the distribution firm, their high participation is seen as significant.

Conversely, the low participation of outside sales, inside sales, and accounting/finance suggests these positions have little influence in the decision to procure off-brands. We would have expected to see more participation from the sales function, as sellers are heavy influencers of new products. However, their input may have been partially offset by a strong showing from Sales Management. Also, off-brands are typically not new products in function or form. Often, they are functional substitutes for existing technologies at a lower price point. Since the price points can be substantially lower, and distribution is a thin return on sales business, the financial impact to the firm is powerful and motivating. To understand just how compelling the price differential can be, we offer the next section, early in the book, to give readers an understanding of why distribution executives are anxious to find out more about off-brands.

Off-Brands and Profit Economics of Durable Goods Distribution

Wholesale distribution is, perennially, a low-profit industry. Before-tax returns of operating profit expressed as a percent of sales typically range between 1.5% and 2.5%, depending on the industry and the business cycle.[1] The profit heuristic for durable goods distributors is that an average distributor will have 2% of sales in before-tax operating profits. And each 1% before tax will produce a return on investment of between 5% and 6%. Or, typically, a 2% of sales operating profit produces an ROI of 10% to 12%. Furthermore, most of the distributor's costs are in inventory. Referring to Figure 2-4, Scenario 1, we find that the typical distributor has 76% of sales in expensed inventory or cost of goods sold (COGS), and the gross profit on sales is 24%.

Figure 2-4 Effects of Differing Levels of Off-Brand Purchases on Distributor Net Income

Income Statement Category	Scenario 1 Historical Status	Scenario 2 10% Off-Brands	Scenario 3 20% Off-Brands	Scenario 3 30% Off-Brands
Sales	100%	100%	100%	100%
Cost of Goods Sold	76%	73.00%	70.00%	68.00%
Gross Margins on Sales	24%	27%	30%	32%
Operating Expenses:				
Management Salaries	3.50%	3.50%	3.50%	3.50%
Outside Sales	4%	4%	4%	4%
Inside Sales	3%	3%	3%	3%
Warehouse Labor and Equipment	2.50%	2.50%	2.50%	2.50%
Shipping Labor and Equipment	2.50%	2.50%	2.50%	2.50%
Accounting/Finance	1%	1%	1%	1%
Purchasing	1%	1%	1%	1%
Rent and Utilities	2.50%	2.50%	2.50%	2.50%
Information Technology	1%	1%	1%	1%
Miscellaneous	1%	1%	1%	1%
Total Operating Expenses	22.00%	22.00%	22.00%	22.00%
Net Operating Profit Before Tax	2.00%	5.00%	8.00%	10.00%

Looking further down the income statement, we have various expense categories, including management salaries, outside sales, inside sales, warehouse labor and expenses, etc. Operating Expenses total 22% of sales and, when deducted from gross margins, yield a profit before tax of 2% of sales. These ratios are, again, typical across much of durable goods distribution. Also, it is important to note that salaries typically count for 65% to 70%

of operating expenses. Many of these salaries are for labor-intensive work like inside sales, accounting, and warehouse receiving, put-away, picking, and shipping. Labor costs are highly variable with volume, which makes it very difficult to successfully leverage fixed costs to drive profitability. In our work, we advise distributors to streamline variable cost processes with lean principles and the latest technology and maximize pricing opportunity as the best means to grow superior profits. Unlike manufacturers, distributors cannot successfully compete by leveraging fixed costs with increasing volume. And because of the step-cost nature of expenses, distributors are sensitive to maximizing gross margin by a reduction in purchase costs.

To understand the impact of purchase costs on distributor profitability, we created Scenarios 2, 3, and 4. In Scenario 2, the Cost of Goods reflects 10% of the inventory as off-brands with a 35% average cost gain over domestic brands.[2] In Scenario 2, the Cost of Goods decreases 3% to 73%, gross margins increase to 27% and pretax income rises to 5% of sales. The similar comparisons in Scenarios 3 and 4 have 20% and 30% of off-brand purchases, respectively, and the corresponding effects on Cost of Goods, Gross Margins, and Pretax Income. While the Pretax Incomes of 8% to 10% of sales are seldom witnessed, the impact of the Scenarios is clear in several ways:

- The effect of lower priced goods on distributor profitability is immediate and substantial.
- Because of the step-cost nature of operating expenses, distributors that are not competitive in purchases can quickly be put at a disadvantage.

The upshot of Figure 2-4 is that distributors literally cannot financially afford to be non-competitive in purchases. This is the primary reason that, for most vertical markets, we see numerous formal and informal cooperatives and a proliferation of global-sourcing master distributors. Distributors are driving the channel to develop intermediaries who can help drive costs out of commodities and keep them competitive for solvency.

Of course, before-tax incomes as depicted in Figure 2-4 are not common for several reasons. First, most channels are efficient in that knowledge is pervasive and immediate. Hence, the purchase prices of goods are well known and low-cost sources are quickly sought out by wholesale buyers. Second, as lower cost sources are found, the ability of any one company to "hide" margins and increase pretax income in the long run is low. Because of the Internet, the prevalence of information concerning low-cost product sources has greatly accelerated the ability of any and every distributor to procure the lowest-cost producer.[3] Once the source is passed through inventory and sold, the price in the marketplace quickly decreases. While companies may try to hold pricing at previous levels, globalization and the Internet combine to make channel costs decrease rather quickly and inefficiencies or inordinately "high" product margins are quickly recognized, prompting customers to move to the lowest cost supplier. Hence, we believe distributor margins will stay at historic levels, and little long-term gain in channel profits will result from purchases of off-brands. What will most likely occur is that channels will lower their costs, consumers and businesses will pay less for commodities, and the global economy will become more efficient by applying gains in purchasing to other knowledge-based technologies in order to increase productivity. Repeating a theme from the Introduction, modern economies compete by becoming more productive and getting costs down with better technology. The decrease in costs gives the buyer the chance to purchase more, relative to their earnings, and we fully believe that off-brands will, in the long-run, allow channel costs to be significantly reduced.

In summation, the demographics for the research are representative of the population of North American durable goods distribution, and the functional responses foretell a keen interest by executive management in off-brands. And because of the closely held, multi-generational structure of distribution companies, executive interests heavily influence the direction of these firms for the long run.

_____

[1] Profit ratios and metrics are taken from Benfield Consulting benchmarks from both client work and industry accounting ratios.

[2] Average price gain of Off-brands versus Domestic Brands ranges between 30% and 40% and for the purpose of comparison, the average of 35% is used.

[3] Benfield S., Griffith, S., "Cowboy Economics In the Durable Goods Supply Chain: The Chisholm Trail to Destruction," White Paper for Progressive Distributor, December 2006, page 4.

CHAPTER three

Going Global in a Flattening World: What the Data Tell Us about the New Realities of Sourcing Activity

As we have noted in our prior research, the convergence of communications, product standards, and shipping methods drives the flattening of supply chains. It matters little today where something is engineered, manufactured, or stocked. What matters is the total cost of acquisition, and, therefore, the elimination of waste in the value chain. Place this within the backdrop of a laissez faire global economy and the 24/7 availability of information, including product standards and market price, and you have a world where the low-cost producer dominates more quickly than ever before. Thomas Friedman's "flat Earth" has arrived in the world of durable goods distribution, and it has arrived with a vengeance.[1] The results of the survey clearly depict a world in which offshore and off-brand sourcing is growing as a result of technological, logistical, and information convergence.

Offshore and Off-Brand Sourcing is Growing and Growing Rapidly

While some 42% of the respondents indicated that they were sourcing less than 10% of their needs from offshore vendors, almost half of the respondents indicated they were obtaining from 10% to more than 30% of their requirements from such sources. Indeed, as shown in Figure 3-1, 17% of the respondents indicated they were obtaining more than 30% of their total requirements from these off-brand and offshore sources.

Figure 3-1 Percent of Offshore Purchases

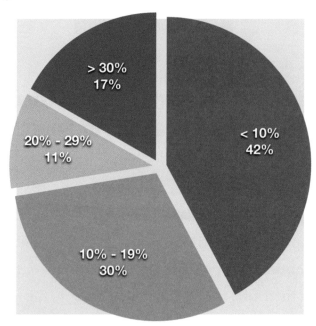

More significantly, 89% of the respondents indicated that their purchases from these sources had increased, and just over half indicated they had "Increased Significantly." Clearly, as shown in Figure 3-2, the trend to offshore sourcing is building momentum within the durable goods distribution space.

Figure 3-2 Offshore Purchase Trend

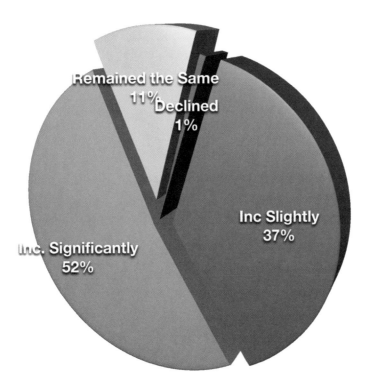

Price is the Major Driving Force

The natural question to ask is "Why is this happening?" The immediate answer is because, in the global economy, it is economically advantageous for purchasers, and it is reliable. For additional detail, we should turn to the question of acquisition cost. Executives responding to the survey indicated, on average, that they enjoyed a price savings of from 21% to 30% when purchasing from offshore sources as compared to traditional, branded, domestic sources for the same items. In many cases, as the figure below shows, the savings were much greater. Twenty-five percent of the executives indicated they saved 31% – 40%, and 14% of them, almost one-seventh, indicated they were saving more than 40% over domestic alternatives. A weighted average price advantage, based on using mid-points of each category, is upwards of

30%. We did not attempt to categorize advantages over 40%. However, in our conversations, there are numerous instances where less complex items offer a 60% to 80% pricing advantage. Using this guideline, the average price advantage is closer to 35%, which we use as a heuristic. Finally, it is important to note that many domestic manufacturers have their products made overseas. And in the question heading, we instructed respondents to include in the domestic brand definition: products that are branded with traditional North American brands, but may be manufactured in plants owned overseas. In short, there is a 35% price advantage from off-brands versus domestic brands that are often made in foreign countries.

Figure 3-3 Offshore Prices Vs Domestic Prices

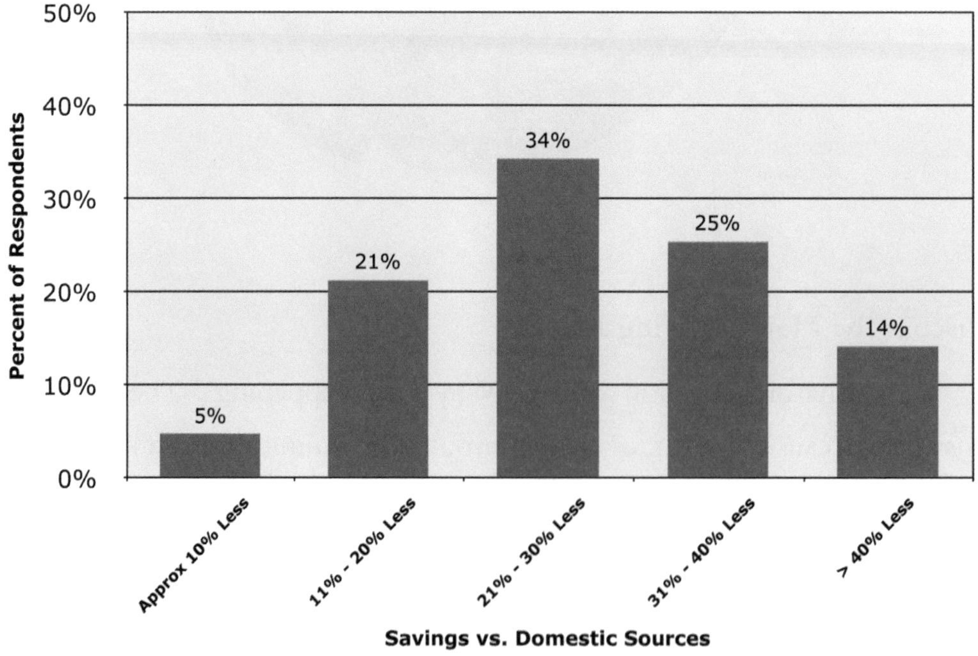

It should come as no surprise that the overwhelming reason cited by executives for developing and using offshore sources was price. When asked for primary reasons for using these sources, respondents indicated, in 90% of their answers, that price was a key motivating factor.

Figure 3-4 Reasons for Offshore Sourcing

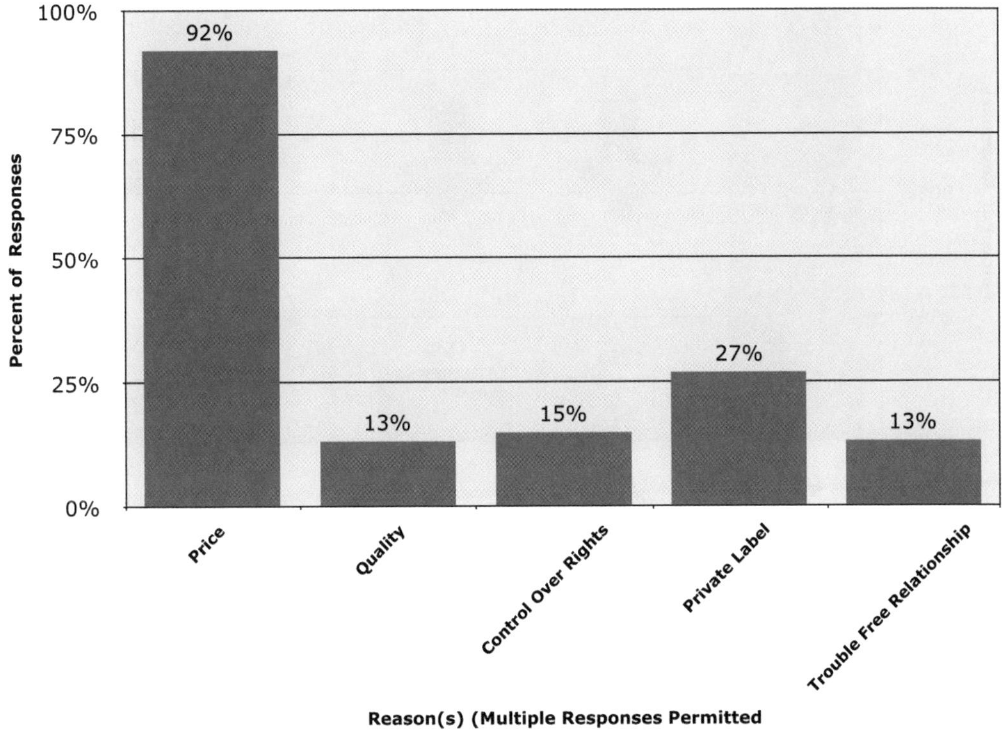

Price Is Not the Only Reason; Quality Also Drives the Decision

However, price was by no means the exclusive reason for sourcing off-brands. Ten percent of the respondents indicated that better quality compared to domestic suppliers was among the reasons for offshore sourcing, while others mentioned increased control over the distribution rights for specific products, the opportunity to private label the products, and a satisfactory, trouble free relationship.

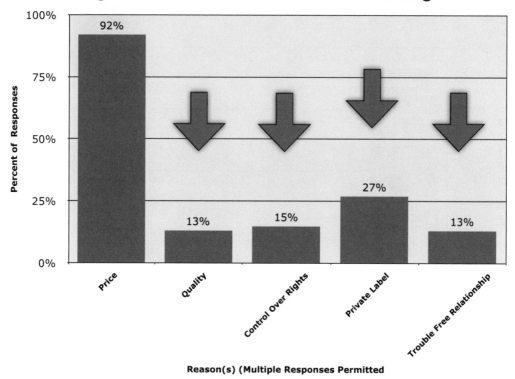

Figure 3-5 Reasons for Offshore Sourcing

Indeed, as shown in Figure 3-6, only some 30% indicated that the quality of foreign, off-brand products was less than that of their domestic counterparts.

Figure 3-6 Foreign Off-Brand Quality Equals or Exceeds Domestic Brands

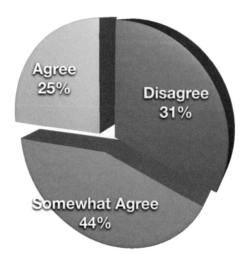

Closely allied to product quality is the issue of product safety and appropriate certifications. Our respondents do not seem unduly worried over this issue. Approximately 64% of them expressed some agreement with the proposition that these overseas manufacturers had obtained adequate certifications and did not pose undue product liability insurance risks.

Figure 3-7 Foreign Off-Brands Have Adequate Certifications and Insurance

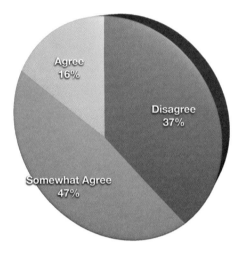

Globalization, it seems, has arrived in the world of the certifying agencies. A quick trip to the Underwriters' Laboratories (UL) website reveals their presence in locations throughout the world, including Taiwan, India, China, Hong Kong, and Korea. Each of these markets is served not only physically, but virtually, with a unique website in the native language. Furthermore, UL has been in many of these countries for a substantial amount of time. Any thought that regulatory, safety, and certification compliance issues would serve as barriers to the encroachment of products from these locations should largely be dismissed as outdated. Despite a spate of product recalls affecting Chinese products, outsourcing remains attractive. There are ample, readily available methods for domestic distributors to reduce the risk of receiving unsatisfactory products. A variety of global firms are available to provide oversight of offshore manufacturing partners. These include London-based Intertek Group plc, which has offices throughout the world (www. intertek.com); Geneva-headquartered SGS SA (www.sgs.com); and Bureau Veritas (www.bureauveritas.com). These firms and others are positioned to provide a variety of quality assurance, testing, inspection, and environmental certification services to reduce the risk of dealing with offshore suppliers.

Figure 3-8 UL China Home Page

Figure 3-9 Intertek Home Page

Figure 3-10 SGS Home Page

Figure 3-11 Bureau Veritas Home Page

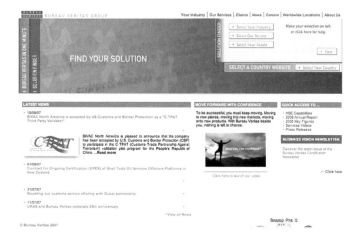

Additionally, we found that many of the sourcing options outside of direct relationships have in-house testing programs or work with various testing and specification agencies. Furthermore, they typically offer product liability and counterfeit coverage for their products. What are these sources, and what is their value to the channel? We asked the respondents and, in the next section, reported the answers. The data so far depicts North American durable goods distributors reacting to increased competitive pressure and declining margins by using globalization to their advantage. Significant numbers are turning to offshore and off-branded sources to secure products that are significantly less costly than their domestic counterparts. This flattening of the world, as Friedman[1] refers to it, is affording distributors, in the short run, an opportunity to retain, if not grow, their sales and margins. The picture for domestic manufacturers is much less comforting. The data indicate that close to 20% of all purchases is now being sourced from these foreign, non-branded sources, and the percentage is growing significantly. Clearly, globalization and the ability to easily access foreign sources of supply are shifting the power in the channel back to the distributor. However, this power shift comes with some significant long-term changes for the distributor that we discuss in later chapters. For now, let us simply say that the traditional domestic manufacturers are no longer adding value to many of these commoditized products. Their value chains contain superfluous and costly components, resulting in prices that are no longer competitive and can no longer be justified.

---

[1] Friedman, T. (2005). *The World Is Flat: A Brief History of the Twenty-First Century*. New York: Farrar, Straus and Giroux.

four

CHAPTER

Cooperatives, Master Distributors, and Buying Groups Add Value

This flattening of the world is clearly making it easier for distributors to source offshore. As shown below, 46% of the responses indicated that the distributors were buying at least a portion of their offshore sourced product directly from foreign manufacturers without the need to engage the services of a master distributor, cooperative, buying group, or other intermediary.

Figure 4-1 Offshore Sources Used

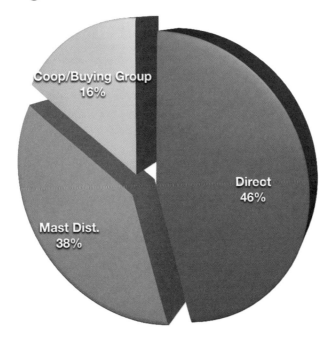

The power of the flat world and the globalization phenomena are more clearly illustrated if we compare the purchasing habits of large distributors (annual revenues of more than $50 million) with those of small distributors, defined as those with annual revenues of less than $20 million. We would expect that larger distributors with, presumably, more access to technology and greater buying power would be much more likely to purchase directly from foreign sources and to avoid intermediaries than smaller distributors. As shown below, this difference is noticeable, but slight.

Figure 4-2 Offshore Sources for Small Distributors

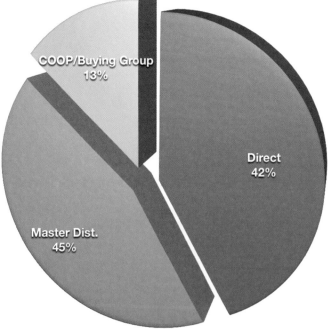

Figure 4-3 Offshore Sources for Large Distributors

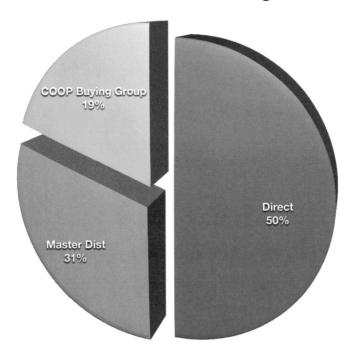

While almost 50% of the responses from the large distributors indicated some direct sourcing, the direct sourcing percentage for small distributors was only slightly smaller, just over 40%.

Probing more deeply, we asked the executives their perception of the value added by cooperatives or informal buying groups when sourcing from offshore vendors. The answers, as shown in Figure 4-4, are clear. Almost 70% of the executives indicated at least partial agreement with the assertion that such arrangements add only limited value when sourcing offshore. Direct relationships and master distributors are a much more prominent source of off-brands than cooperatives or informal alliances. However, as we will explore later in the text, cooperatives, either independent or informal buying groups, and importers are expected to grow as demand for off-brands grows. These entities have varying value bundles, and there are six distinct sources for off-brands that will be explored in future chapters.

Figure 4-4 Cooperatives and Buying Groups Add Limited Value When Sourcing Off-Brands

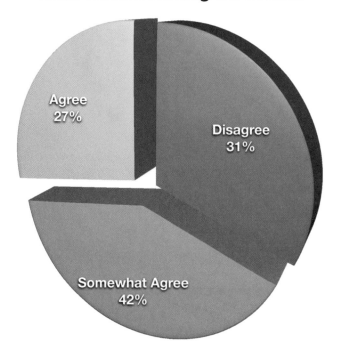

Even the smaller distributors, which are typically disadvantaged in terms of buying power and channel power, can leverage technology and globalization to act like big companies. We believe this is due, in part, to the rise of firms dedicated to the task of simplifying the logistics challenges brought on by foreign sourcing. Both FedEx and UPS have developed a panoply of services aimed at helping even the small firm meet these challenges. For example, they both offer comprehensive solutions from freight consolidation in China; to LCL container freight; to UPS' Direct-to-Store service, which will consolidate shipments in the country of origin, ship via sea or air freight, handle customs and duties, deconsolidate the shipments, and deliver the required portions directly to distributor branches, distribution centers or, when specified, directly to customers. As Tom Peters[1] noted as long ago as 1997, "Distance is dead." And while we try to avoid such comprehensive statements, if distance is not dead, it is becoming much less of a significant factor in the durable goods channel.

Foreign manufacturers appear to have recognized this trend as well. Distributors generally agree with the proposition that these offshore sources desire direct relationships with customers without the complication of intermediaries. Only when these intermediaries offer a clear value advantage to direct relationships are they considered viable alternatives. And, again, given the newness and flux of the trend toward off-brands, we expect that intermediaries will increase and specialize in product service bundles as commerce patterns become established.

Figure 4-5 Off-Brands Prefer Direct Relationships

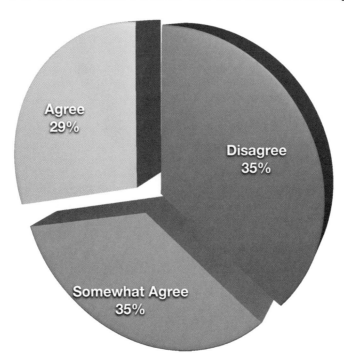

In the broad meaning of Friedman's[2] flat world, the playing field is being leveled, and small firms with judicious use of technology have access to the advantages of off-brands and can compete like big firms. More significantly for manufacturers, even these smaller distributors are successfully shifting the power in the channel away from the domestic brand manufacturers where it has resided for many years. When specifically asked to predict the future distribution of power in their channel, distributor executives indicated they see a significant reduction in the channel power held by the traditional manufacturers and brands. As shown below, only 13% did not share this view.

Figure 4-6 Domestic Brands Will Lose Channel Power

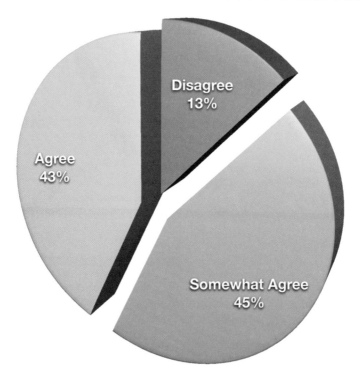

Globalization has allowed distributors to take advantage of purchasing options and supplier choices they have not previously had. Should you need convincing, we urge you to "Google" the term "pipe fittings China" and note the number of readily available sources eager to supply U.S. firms. Alternatively, enter the address http://www.alibaba.com/countrysearch/ CN-suppliers/Pipe_Fitting.html into your browser and peruse page after page of products available from suppliers touting adherence to international standards and ready availability at attractive prices. Similar experiences await many commoditized products.

These data begin to reveal the decreasing relevance of the buying cooperative, a mechanism often seen as one way for the small distributor to level the playing field by equalizing the purchasing-cost advantage typically held by its bigger competitors. Clearly, as the chart below illustrates, distributors both large and small are bypassing cooperatives and buying groups in their quest for more cost-effective sources, as these intermediaries are slow to accept the realities of globalization. Some 57% of the respondents *who indicated they used buying groups* told the authors that these groups had failed to offer offshore and off-brand products as alternatives to the domestic products traditionally offered.

Figure 4-7 Co-Op/Buying Group Offshore Activity

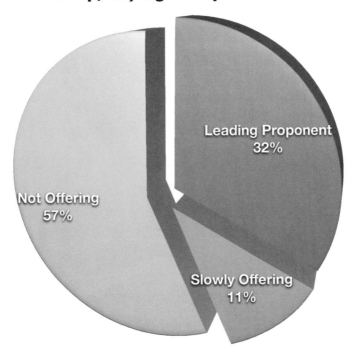

The message here seems clear. These buying groups and cooperatives are often loath to upset the relationships they have developed with domestic-branded manufacturers. More importantly, they add limited value to a global supply chain wherein even a small distributor can seek out a foreign source, negotiate a very favorable price on even a modest volume of purchases, and quickly receive and remarket the products at enhanced margins. In short, they are adding limited value to the global value chain. Only in instances where the cooperative is pursuing off-brands for their membership are they assured of a place in the global economy. Some notable buying groups have, predictably, launched off-brand efforts. We expect these efforts to grow to the extent the cooperatives can delineate a clear, understandable value picture.

In summary, we see a convincing picture of increased globalization in the durable goods distribution business. Distributors report that the cost advantages are too great to ignore. Their offshore purchases are significant and growing, the flattening world of global logistics and communications are bringing change to buying groups and similar arrangements, and, most importantly, a growing level of customer acceptance of these products. It is not hard to understand why, as depicted below, distributors are actively seeking out such sourcing arrangements.

Figure 4-8 Distributors Actively Seeking Relationships With Offshore Suppliers

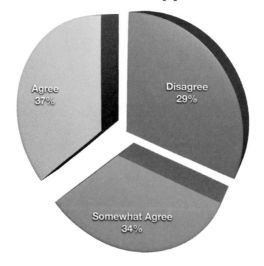

End Customer and Vendor Reactions

We would be remiss if we did not include research on end customer and vendor reactions. The off-brand trend, while strong and financially necessary, would not be possible unless end customers found the products were on a par with the quality of domestic brands. To understand the acceptability of off-brands to the existing distributor customer, we asked about their reactions to off-brands versus domestic brands. The question had four choices, with one choice per respondent allowed. The choices and percent of responses were:

- Customers readily accept off-brands without question - 19.6%
- Customers accept some off-brands but not others - 28%
- Customers would rather buy domestic brands, even if they were made in foreign countries - 8.9%
- Customers will try off-brands because they offer a good price at acceptable quality - 43.5%

Figure 4-9 Distributor Perception of Customer Reaction to Off-Brand Products

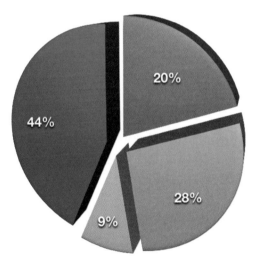

- ● Readily Accept
- ◔ Accept Some, But Not All
- ◯ Cust. Desire Domestic Brands Regardless of Place of Mfg.
- ● Will Try - Better Price at Acceptable Quality

The responses contained in Figure 4-9 depict a customer base that, for the most part, will readily try and accept off-brands if the buying experience is good. A substantial 44% indicated they would give the off-brand products a try. Our estimate is that if the trial is successful, the customer will move toward the off-brand as long as the pricing is attractive for doing so. The statement that customers would readily accept off-brands at close to a 20% response is significant also. Our conclusion is that off-brands and foreign-manufactured goods have become more commonplace in North America and are readily accepted. Finally, the response for domestic brand preference was lowest at 8.9%. This is in sync with other questions about the falling popularity of domestic brands.

Actual end user research on off-brand acceptance is more difficult to find. However, in 2007, Ray and Gordon did an end-user-based survey for the electrical industry on foreign-manufactured goods. The average brand apathy, across 18 product categories, was 31%. In essence, approximately one-third of the electrical wholesalers' customers were apathetic when it came to brand, with price and supplier service being more important choices to drive purchase decision. In addition, the research pointed to contractors using a generic product description 44% of the time when ordering, which would give an advantage to off-brands. And, 84% of contractors said their distributors allowed for product substitution. This practice would give new users a chance for trial of the off-branded product, which is crucial to establishing the viability of foreign goods.

In closing this chapter, we felt it important to understand the reaction of domestic brands when they discovered distributors were replacing their products with off-brands. Many domestic manufacturer relationships have been ongoing for generations, and it is important to understand how the vendor base reacted to the loss of sales. We asked distributors what happened to domestic vendors when they discovered foreign goods. There were four choices to the question, with one choice per respondent. The choices and their percentage responses (Figure 4-10) were:

- Our domestic vendors don't realize we are sourcing off-brands until their sales drop precipitously - 20%

- Vendors escalate conflict once they find we are sourcing off-brands - 21%
- Vendors approach the situation carefully and with restraint once they find we are sourcing off-brands - 57%
- Vendors immediately sign up a competitive distributor once they find we are sourcing off-brands - 2%

Figure 4-10 Perceived Domestic Vendor Reaction

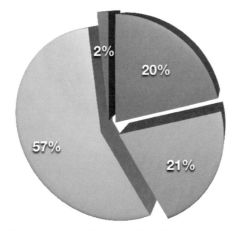

● Vendors Don't Realize sourcing Change Until Sales Drop
● React With Hostility and Escalate coflict
● Approach With Restraint; Investigate Actions Needed to Improve Relationshp
● Sign up Competitive Distributor

It would appear that domestic vendors approach off-brands with the proverbial "cool-headed" strategy, work toward understanding why they are losing sales, and work with the distributor to revamp their relationship. The success attained in improving the relationship and regaining sales is unknown to us, but unless the domestic vendor can match off-brand pricing or give the distributor financial incentive to stay, it is likely that they have lost their position on the distributor's warehouse shelf for a long time. Of interest was the response indicating that slightly over 20% of vendors react with hostility and escalate conflict. This tactic, in our experience, almost never works and typically impairs the distributor relationship in the long run. Even if the off-brand doesn't work out and the displaced domestic vendor is a viable option, the distress and resentment over escalating conflict typically causes the distributor to seek alternative sources. For the domestic vendor, escalating channel conflict is rarely a good idea. Distributors are privately held, and key managers can have tenures lasting decades. Like the bull elephant, their memories last a long time.

---

[1] Peters, T. (1997). *The Circle of Innovation*. New York: Vintage.

[2] Friedman, T. (2005). *The World Is Flat: A Brief History of the Twenty-First Century*. New York: Farrar, Straus and Giroux.

CHAPTER five

The Role and Impact of Channel Services and Pre/Post Product Supports

Channel support services and post-sales service are important elements in the purchase decision for durable goods. Hence, the research would be incomplete without measuring and ranking the manufacturer service provision for domestic brands and off-brands. Channel support services include a variety of necessary and value adding events to support the product and enhance financial performance. Channel supports can also be expensive, averaging 30% or more of all channel costs.[1] For the survey, we gauged the importance and quality of service provision for fifteen of the more common channel services including:

- Timely Delivery
- Complete Delivery
- EDI Capabilities
- Field Sales
- Technical Support
- Marketing Programs
- Product Literature
- Warranty Return Privileges
- Payment Terms

- Product Application Training
- Accurate Invoicing
- Timely Credits
- Volume Rebates
- Quality and Variety of Packaging
- Certification and Code Approvals

We made no attempt to define the services in the body of the questions. They are ubiquitous and well understood across durable goods markets.

For each service as provided by their vendors, we asked respondents to choose from one of three levels of importance, including "Somewhat Important," "Important," or "Very Important." Our logic in doing this was that if the service was unimportant, it would not have been a staple in the vendors' arsenal(s). Some of the services are wrapped around the product at the time of transaction, including delivery and packaging, payment terms, and accurate invoicing, while others go into the product before it is shipped, such as literature and certification and code approvals. Finally, some of the services are not specific to the physical transfer of the product and are most valued as pre- and post-sales support. These services include EDI capabilities, field sales, technical support, product application training, warranty/return privileges, credits, and volume rebates.

The survey results are condensed in the chart in Figure 5-1. In the figure, we list the service and the percentage of respondents by category of "Somewhat Important," "Important," or "Very Important."

Figure 5-1

Service	Service Importance Ranked In Descending Order by Index			Service Importance Index (VI +I)-SWI
	Somewhat Important	Important	Very Important	
Timely Delivery	7.70%	36.30%	56%	84.60%
Accurate Invoices	8.10%	33.10%	59%	83.80%
Timely Credits	13.30%	45.80%	41%	73.50%
Warranty Return Privileges	17.00%	41.50%	41%	65.40%
Complete Delivery	19.40%	41.80%	38.80%	61.20%
Certification and Code Approvals	23.50%	29%	47.50%	53.00%
Payment Terms	30.70%	41.50%	41%	51.70%
Technical Support	26.90%	41.30%	31.70%	46.10%
Quality and Variety of Packaging	32.10%	43.50%	24.40%	35.80%
Volume Rebates	33.10%	31.30%	35.50%	33.70%
Product Literature	46.30%	38.40%	15.20%	7.30%
Product Application Training	51.20%	34.10%	14.60%	-2.50%
Field Sales	54%	31.10%	14.90%	-8.00%
Marketing Programs	61.40%	31.30%	7.20%	-22.90%
EDI Capabilities	85.50%	14.50%	0%	-71.00%

In the far right, we developed an Importance Index, which is simply the formula of: (Very Important + Important) - Somewhat Important. The contents of the figure are ranked in descending order of the Importance Index Value. The most important service, as scored by the index, is timely delivery, followed by accurate invoices, timely credits, warranty return privileges, complete delivery, certification and code approvals, payment terms, and technical support. Quality and variety of packaging and volume rebates scored, as indexed, in the 30% range, and the remaining five services had low or negative indices. These were product literature (7.3%), product application training (-2.5%), field sales (-8%), marketing programs (-22%), and EDI capabilities (-71%).

The Service Importance Index is pertinent to the understanding of how distributors value services. Both distributors and manufacturers can use the Index and rankings to help evaluate products and vendors and to determine whether monies spent on channel supports are being used for the services that add the most value. The services that have low or negative rankings should be scrutinized and, if they are not yielding value commensurate with their funding, should be scaled back. To understand how off-brands' quality of service provisions compare with domestic brands, we asked questions about the fifteen previous services. The comparison of off-brand services versus domestic-brand services is important because it gives a picture of the service vulnerabilities of either party, and this can be used to guide channel members in aligning services with what the market will bear.

Service Comparisons and Service Gaps

We asked the respondents to compare service quality using a multiple-choice scale of: "Not as Good," "Equal To," or "Better Than." The respondents were limited to one choice per service comparison, and the question involved comparing off-brand service quality to domestic brands. The results are seen by service in Figure 5-2. In general, we believe that if off-brand services are comparable to domestic brands in the percentage of scores in the "Better Than" and "Equal To" categories, then the price differential of 35% and reasonable quality will tilt the buying decision to the off-brand. In the figure, we created a Provision Index, which is simply the score of "Better Than" plus "Equal To," less the score of "Not as Good." As long as the index score was zero or higher, then the off-brand had a good chance of being favored over the domestic brand. Looking at the Provision Index column, we see off-brands score higher in the areas of accurate invoices, timely credits, complete delivery, payment terms, quality and variety of packaging, volume rebates, certification and code approvals, warranty/return privileges, and timely delivery. Off-brands score less than domestic brands on the Provision Index for the services of product literature, technical support, EDI capabilities, product application training, field sales, and marketing programs.

To understand the impact of the scores versus their importance, we added the final column to the figure (from Figure 5-1), which is labeled "Service Importance Index." Comparing the two columns yields the following:

- For the important services of accurate invoices down to code and certification approvals, off-brands do quite well compared to domestic brands.

- For warranty returns, timely delivery and technical support, off-brands score slightly better than domestic brands, but the services are of high importance, and the "Not as Good" scores were substantial. This could be an advantage for the domestic brands. We highlighted these scores in green.

- Product literature scored better for domestic brands, but the service is of relatively low importance, and this is not seen as a disadvantage for off-brands.

- Domestic brands scored high in the areas of EDI capabilities, product application training, field sales, and marketing programs.

- The high-score services of domestic brands are relatively unimportant to distributors and as compared to other services. These are highlighted in red in the figure.

The most surprising part of the service research is exhibited in the red-highlighted cells in Figure 5-2.

Figure 5-2

Service	Not As Good	Equal	Better Than	Provision Index (BT + E)-NAG	Service Importance Index
Accurate Invoices	6.80%	85.20%	8%	86.40%	83.80%
Timely Credits	18.90%	71.30%	10%	62.20%	73.50%
Complete Delivery	21.70%	53.40%	24.80%	56.50%	61.20%
Payment Terms	21.90%	67.50%	10.6%	56.20%	51.70%
Quality and Variety of Packaging	28.20%	60.70%	11.00%	43.50%	35.80%
Volume Rebates	30.70%	46.90%	22.80%	39.00%	33.70%
Certification and Code Approvals	31.30%	62%	6.90%	37.50%	53.00%
Warranty Return Privileges	43.70%	51.90%	4%	12.60%	65.40%
Timely Delivery	47.00%	39.00%	14%	6.00%	84.60%
Product Literature	57.40%	39.50%	3.10%	-14.80%	7.30%
Technical Support	67.90%	28.40%	3.70%	-35.80%	46.10%
EDI Capabilities	68.20%	31.20%	0.600%	-36.40%	-71%
Product Application Training	74.50%	23.60%	1.90%	-49.00%	-2.50%
Field Sales	75.2%	21.10%	3.70%	-50.40%	-8%
Marketing Programs	75.30%	21.50%	3.20%	-50.60%	-22.90%

The services of product application training, field sales, marketing programs, and product literature were considered far more advanced in domestic brands than those offered by off-brands. However, as shown in Figure 5-1, these four services were the lowest scoring in service importance. Could it be that domestic manufacturers are investing in services that are relatively unimportant to the industrial buying decision? And if so, what are the costs of these services, and do they further exacerbate the price differential between off-brands and domestic brands? We willl reveal our thoughts on this in the next section.

Are Domestic Manufacturers Overinvesting in Services?

Product Life Cycle Management as a managerial subject and discipline has been addressed in American business literature since the 1960s.[2] Seminal articles by Ted Levitt of the Harvard Business School and George Day of Wharton[3] urged manufacturers to go beyond the conceptual framework of the Product Life Cycle (PLC) to practical application of its principles, including its use as a tool for evaluating the investment in service supports. Sadly, we believe that there has been a dearth of research in and much forgetfulness concerning industrial marketing topics and principles, including PLC management, in the last 10 to 15 years. As a discipline, industrial marketing isn't found in the syllabi at many graduate business schools. Consequently, this educational and managerial dismissal of fundamental industrial marketing knowledge contributes to the research findings that show an overinvestment in support services by domestic manufacturers.

To be fair, the lack of industrial marketing education isn't the sole reason for the dilemma that domestic brands find themselves in. As products age and their sales numbers grow, they are attended by a host of important services, including field sales, product knowledge, literature, and application training. Growth products need these services to reach their market potential and to maintain their market position. They are handmaidens to profit maximization. At the onset of the mature stage in the PLC, management still finds the ongoing revenue streams worthy of most of these supports. The majority of manufacturers find that, in mature markets, services become differentiators, and reducing service support can be dangerous and may even precipitate share loss. However, many industrial products are well past the onset of the mature stage and, if not in decline, are aged to the point of commoditization where price or, more correctly, low-cost manufacturing wins. We believe that cultural inertia of product-centric or sales-centric marketing, which develops and supports products in the growth stage and cements position in the early mature stage, too often outlive their investment horizon. Technical sellers and engineers dominate industrial product companies, but wrapping these expensive services around commodity products makes poor investment sense and can place the basic product at a competitive disadvantage. We are quite sure that the survey results point this out. It is quite possible that foreign manufacturers use the propensity of service overinvestment as a rationale for market entry or rely on it as a competitive disadvantage in attacking domestic brands.

The essential question from the preceding argument is: just how much do domestic brands invest in support services that aren't necessarily valued by the channel? We cannot find definitive research on the question. However, based on our combined 50 years in industrial markets and including information from consulting records, we offer the following ranges of service investment, as a percent of sales, for the service(s) of:

- Field sales: 1% to 3% of sales
- Marketing programs including co-op dollars: 0.5% to 2% of sales
- Product literature: 0.1% to 0.5% of sales
- Product training: 0.5% to 1% of sales

For manufacturers, the average expenditure on these services can be upwards of 4% to 5% of sales or 20% to 25% of operating expenses. While this amount won't totally eliminate the 35% pricing gap with off-brands, it is an important part of the cost disadvantage experienced by domestic brands. We would also note that blindly decreasing the investment in these services is not the answer. Manufacturers with distributors need to engage in strategic discussions on where and how to deploy funds for products. The need for solid process management and judicious investment is key. If domestic brands begin to financially rationalize service expenditures, there will be important implications for existing channels. We spend some time in the closing section discussing these changes.

Channel Change Scenarios: Domestic Brand Decrease in Channel Funding

Domestic manufacturers spend considerable market development funds in industrial channels, including trade shows, cooperative funds, and support and training of distributors and end users. In our practices, we have worked with dozens of industry associations, and it is almost impossible to find associations that aren't heavily supported by manufacturer funds.

If domestic manufacturers begin to rationalize these investments, as the research suggests they should, there will be significant changes in industrial channels. The most common scenarios are listed below:

- Expect co-op funds to decrease or to have stricter rules of usage. As manufacturers rationalize the funding of commodities and relate them to share loss from off-brands, the monies will be less available or have more restricted usage.
- Expect sales force expenditures to fall. In 2006, we released a research-based book on the need for distributors to makes sales efforts more productive.[4] It appears from our research that domestic manufacturers will need to trim sales efforts as well. While this is not comforting for manufacturer-direct sales forces, agents, and representatives, it is a necessary event, given the research results and gains by off-brands.
- Expect association-sponsored trade shows to receive less funding. Many association events are heavily funded by manufacturers, and many of these events are gathering points for manufacturers and distributors to discuss yearly plans. As they lose position to off-brands, domestic manufacturers will be forced to make a decision regarding their continued support of trade shows and association events. They must decide whether to conserve money and do less costly planning and distributor support. Conversely, expect associations to acknowledge off-brands as members, associate members, or contributors.

In general, we see escalating channel conflict between domestic manufacturers, distributors, associations and cooperatives in the future, and we don't necessarily believe the conflict will be mitigated by "getting everyone together and talking about the issues." In our experience, these administrative or political attempts to limit the conflict often make things worse.

Distributors will also be forced to rationalize their support of domestic brands and support services. Many channel funds are cooperative in nature, requiring equal and authenticated investment by distributors. This matching or "dollar for dollar" funding will come under increased scrutiny by distributors and powerful cooperatives. In some instances, distributors may deploy domestic manufacturing funds to drive customers to off-brands. While "bait and switch" tactics are illegal, particularly when they constitute fraudulent and deceptive sales practices and include intentional understocking,[5] the current environment of excessive funding by domestic brands and price disparity with off-brands is fertile ground for this to occur. Barring any deceptive use of manufacturer funds, we expect distributors to follow domestic manufacturer leads and trim investment in services that are no longer useful for commodity products or that have outlived their ability to generate income.

We will discuss manufacturer and distributor solution sets to these issues in coming chapters. We encourage all channel members to consider the research and their investment in channel services and whether or not the investment is warranted in financial and strategic terms.

———————

[1] Benfield, S., Baynard, J. *Services That Sell*, 1999, 2004, NAW Publications, Introduction.

[2] Levitt, T., "Exploit the Product Life Cycle," HBR, vol. 43, Nov./Dec., 1965, pp. 81-94.

[3] Day, G., "The Product Life Cycle: Analysis and Application" *Journal of Marketing*, Autumn 1981, vol. 45, pp. 60-67.

[4] Benfield, S, Vurva R., *Restructuring the Distribution Sales Effort*, Brown Books Publishing, 2006.

[5] Wilkie, W., Mela C., Gundlach, G., "Does Bait and Switch Really Benefit Consumers…," *Marketing Science,* vol. 17, no. 3, 1998, pp. 290-293.

CHAPTER six

Why Domestic Manufacturer Brands Are Declining

Marketing texts and research are filled with treatises on the subject of developing and perpetuating the power of the brand. Brand power can be described as being "first in the mind"[1] The idea is that a strong brand name and position, supported by a quality product or service, has equity in that it is recognizable. Because of this position in the mind, the brand is like an annuity. In essence, the end user simply goes back to the tried and true brand because it is reliable, and it works.

Like most generalized statements, this one is most applicable to specific circumstances. The power of the brand and its vaunted position in the mind work best in the initial stages of a product's life. Why? For industrial products where quality and performance are key, a reliable brand substantially reduces risk. For instance, in the water well industry of two decades ago, the Well King brand of pressurized well tanks was highly sought after by installers and distributors. One of the key factors for this was the reliability of their products and the lack of call-backs a pump installer would have to make.[2] Following its introduction in the early 1960s, Well King brand dominated the shelves of pump distributors well into the 1980s. However, by the mid-1980s, reliable competitive brands that had better price points began appearing, and by

2006, the parent company, American Well Works Inc., filed for bankruptcy protection. What happened? While there were many reasons for the company's inability to meet its financial obligations in 2006, from the perspective of those who sold the Well King brand during the 1980s and into the '90s, there is a general opinion that the parent company "milked" the brand for far too long. In essence, the company rode the coattails of the Well King brand without sufficiently investing in the ongoing technological performance enhancements to justify a significantly higher price point. Additionally, there were numerous new products that were financially disappointing. Over time, competitors were able to copy its technology and produce a reliable product at lower prices. The result was a gradual degradation in financial performance of a parent company that had squandered its technological lead and brand franchise.

The story of the Well King brand is a fitting example of what is happening to numerous domestic industrial brands with recognizable and seemingly stable positions in the mind. These brands began in the early years of their industries. For all intents and purposes, they followed the rise of the industrial revolution and the development of modern technologies, including transportation, construction, automation, and manufacturing industries. At the beginning of any industry, there are any number of products and brands vying for a finite market. Over time, however, the number of lasting brands typically sifts down to a handful of contenders that vigorously compete for a few points of market share. Over time, these technologies become established, developing engineering and performance standards that are well known and published and which act as industry entrance requirements for competitors.

Looking at the research, we find that the power of many established brands is clearly on the decline. From Figure 6-1, approximately 60% of the respondents agreed with the statement that "Brand recognition…" is "losing value."

Figure 6-1 Distributor View of Brand Importance

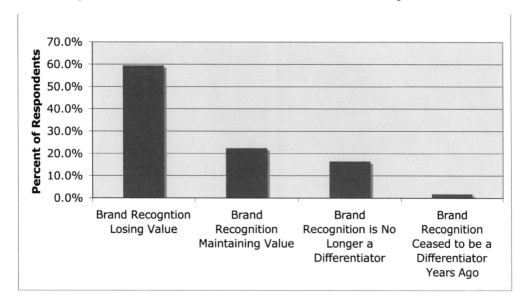

Slightly over 20% of the respondents chose the statement "brand recognition is maintaining value" and an equal number of respondents chose the statements "brand recognition is no longer a differentiator" or "brand recognition ceased to be a differentiator years ago." The seminal question is why is the brand losing value? Our simple answer is that the domestic brand simply costs too much. In Figure 6-2, we questioned the respondents as to why they felt domestic brands, even if they were manufactured overseas, were not cost-competitive. The question allowed for multiple responses, but the responses and their relative percentages were:

- Expensive management - 26%
- Euthanizing the brand - 11%
- Rewarding the shareholder with excess rewards - 24%
- Domestic brands out of touch with their value proposition - 39%

Figure 6-2 Perceived Reasons for Excess Cost

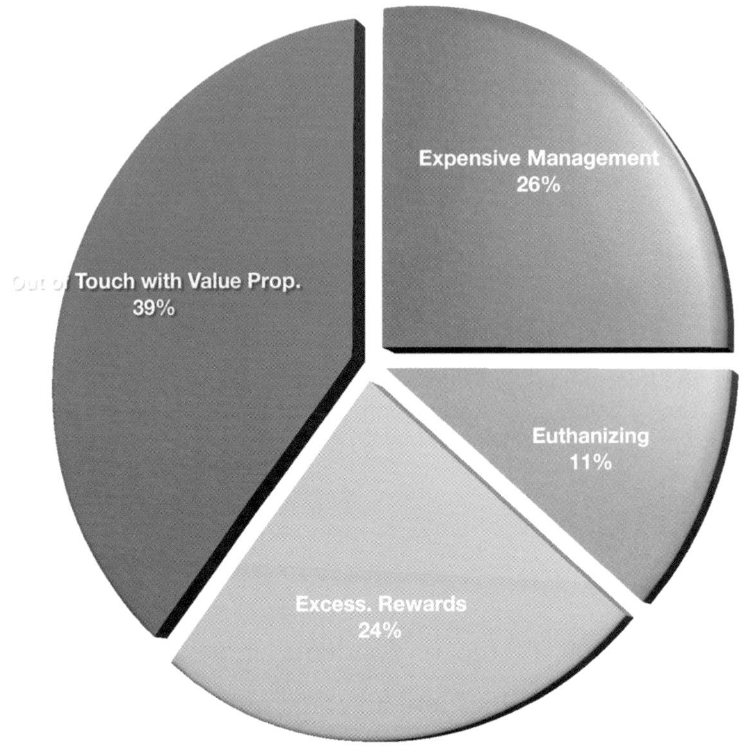

While many domestic brands locate their manufacturing plants overseas, their executive, marketing, and research and development functions are often stateside. When we look at these functions versus foreign off-brand counterparts, the disparities in pay are, to say the least, staggering. For instance, the top tier of U.S. manufacturing executives earns 475 times the wage of an average employee. In industrialized European economies, this metric varies from 13 to 24 times more.[3] When it comes to research and development, the costs, while not as lopsided, are still significantly more. Most research and development is done by engineers who are charged with developing new technologies, extending product life of existing technologies, or testing and updating technical specifications. Recent research on domestic engineers' salaries finds that they are 40% to 80% higher than their counterparts in foreign countries.[4] Therefore, it appears that when 26% of the respondents chose "expensive management" as a reason for the decline of the domestic brand, they were accurate.

Brand recognition, brand loyalty, and their annuities are powerful forces. The temptation to lean on an established brand of yesteryear, raise prices, and atrophy in the development of new revenue streams with better products and services is common. We call this "euthanizing the brand," which is a phrase used to describe the slow death of a brand from excessive price increases and diminishing investment. While the statement only attracted 11% of the respondents, the response is significant in that, due to multiple responses, the question has a statistically valid sample size. Other reasons for the decline of domestic brands (excess shareholder rewards and unsupported value propositions) in many ways feed the noncompetitive posture of domestic brands.

The U.S. economy is a high-cost/high-performance economy that has seen historical returns on equities in the 12% per annum range over the past half century.[5] The past history of returns requires ongoing and quarterly improvement in financial performance. Other economies have not established historical returns that approach that of U.S. companies, and other cultures do not necessarily require quarterly improvement. Because of this, off-brands made on foreign shores often require a lower standard of financial performance and/or are supported by a cultural appetite for lower returns in the early years of an investment. Hence, while companies returning 12% average annually may not be excessive in the U.S. historical view, the double-digit return is often excessive for other cultures and emerging industrial economics. The low returns of emerging economies would, on the surface, indicate that these countries and companies have trouble accessing capital markets. However, given the manufacturing cost advantage of off-brands, the long-term return on investment outweighs the short-term mentality of the U.S. financial community. Therefore, the access to capital for foreign manufacturers with low-cost manufacturing is quite good.

Largely because of the previously cited issues of expensive management, euthanizing the brand, and excess shareholder rewards, domestic companies have in many instances divorced the value of the brand from a reasonable price in the marketplace. Often we find that domestic companies have "milked the brand" for years to prop up returns or to invest in ventures that did not meet reasonable financial goals. Over time, the brand equity declines as competitors chip away at the high price of the dominant brand. And over time and rather insidiously, the dominant brand and its management becomes more dependent on an overly high-priced market position as the company either has not engendered a culture that creates new value streams or has atrophied in developing better technologies at lower costs. If the brand is "euthanized" because of corporate neglect in developing and managing value, the metaphorical nails are often in the brand "coffin" long before the corporation acknowledges it. Even if the acknowledgement of the situation is complete, the corporate parent must use—or, more accurately, *abuse*—the remaining brand equity to keep the doors open until new value streams are found. The rate at which the value of a brand erodes begins as a slow, barely perceptible decline, reaches a tipping point, then drops precipitously. In the Well King example, many sellers and marketers of the brand felt, by the late 1980s, that the value proposition of the brand was out of sync with its price. It took nearly 20 years for the parent company, American Well Works, to file for bankruptcy protection, however, and the final decline into insolvency in 2006 came abruptly and surprised many in the marketplace.[6]

Long-Term Distributor Trends for Off-Brands

We don't want to be alarmist about the future of longstanding domestic brands. Indeed, many domestic manufacturers have moved plants off-shore, reduced costs, and have highly competitive brands from yesteryear. However, many domestic companies have not made the necessary strides to compete on a global best-cost basis, and the long-term purchasing trends for these companies is not encouraging. We asked distributors what their five year purchase trend should be. The results are captured in Figure 6-3. In the figure, there were four possible responses, and the responses and their percentages are as follows:

- Accelerate purchases from various sources - 40%
- Accelerate purchases through a direct relationship with a foreign manufacturer - 25%
- Remain about the same in off-brand purchases - 33%
- Decrease purchases of off-brand items - 2%

Figure 6-3 Future Offshore Purchasing Trends

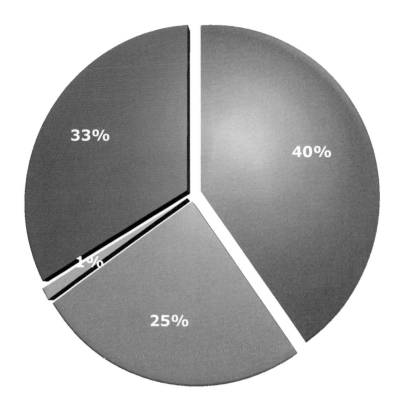

- Accelerate Purchases From Various Sources
- Accelerate Purchases From Foreign Manufacturer
- Decrease Buying From Various Sources
- Decrease Buying From Foreign Manufacturer

In the first bullet, "various sources" refers to global master distributors, cooperatives, and buying groups where off-brands are often sourced. The number of companies that will accelerate purchases of off-brands either through middlemen or directly from foreign manufacturers is 65% of the respondent base. Interestingly, one third of the respondents did not foresee a substantial change in off-brand purchases, and 2% of the respondents said they would "decrease purchases of off-brand items." Clearly, the long-term trend for purchases of off-brands is predominant, and this does not bode well for established domestic brands. The future for domestic brands is not altogether bleak. There are several strategic options, and we explored those in the survey.

We asked respondents what domestic manufacturers and brands should do to combat off-brands. The question offered multiple choices, and respondents were asked to pick the one that most closely applied to their experience. The responses and their percentages can be seen in Figure 6-4.

Figure 6-4 To Combat the Threat, Domestic Mfg. Should...

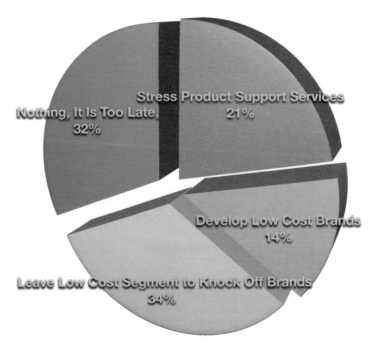

Twenty-one percent of the respondents suggested "stressing product support services." In some instances, where product support is critical to the application and key to the buying decision, a domestic manufacturer could beef up support services and salvage the brand. Typically, this is found in complex technology products or applications where the product is central to a capital intensive process. Thirteen percent suggested that domestic manufacturers develop low-cost brands, while 33% of the respondents suggested development of new applications and leaving the low-cost brands to foreign manufacturers. While new applications and new markets may be feasible for some manufactures, most cannot simply negate their longstanding brands to the foreign competition. Why? Many of the original product platforms for domestic companies still contribute to the long-run fixed costs of the firm. Simply leaving the mature product platform to low-cost foreign alternatives would mean immediate financial hardship. While we argue that, without a low cost global position, domestic firms face hardship, the statement is positioned toward the long run. Simply giving up mature products to foreign low-cost alternatives can best be termed "suicidal." Finally, 33% of the respondents chose the statement "If domestic suppliers don't have a competitive strategy, there is nothing they can do; it is too late." The options for domestic manufacturers and their brands are limited. New products, new applications, developing low-cost brands, or seeking service value in the channel are the suggested competitive stances. None of these options provides a final solution to the need for a globally competitive platform and the ability of distributors to buy foreign brands. Domestic manufacturers will need to carefully consider their options for a competitive stance. We dedicate later chapters of this book to modeling these options.

[1]   Ries, A. and Trout, J., *The 22 Immutable Laws of Marketing*, Harper Business, 1993, pg. 15.

[2]   Benfield, Scott, experience as a manufacturer's representative, with American Well Works and Well King brand, 1982-1986. Company name and brand disguised to protect company identity.

[3]   Judt, Tony, "Europe vs. America," *New York Review of Books*, Vol. 52, No. 2, February 10, 2005, pg. 3.

[4]   Kendrick, Carol, "Outsourcing: The Cause of Lower Salaries for US Engineers?" Outsourcing Issues weblog, October 21, 2006.

[5]   Ferris, R.A., *All About Asset Allocation*, 2006. Excerpted, Fair Use Blog, "Investing in U.S. Equities," 2007.

[6]   As of mid 2007, American Well Works, Inc., had announced successful restructuring of debt. The company maintains an active website that lists employees and ongoing operations. The current status of the company, market position, and rebuilding efforts are unknown.

CHAPTER seven

Facing the Future of the Brands

Distributor Option for Brand Development

As domestic brands decline, there are often opportunities for development of brand identities by channel members. We call this the "ascension" of channel brands, and it follows the movement of channel power from manufacturing to distribution. As industrial channels have matured, power and value have moved to sourcing and delivering the products. While technology and manufacturing are important, they take a back seat to the channel functions involved in getting the product to market.

Branding may or may not be appropriate. It largely depends on the value of the brand in differentiating the product(s). For instance, commodity products such as pipe fittings, electrical outlets, basic fasteners, etc., often do not go by brand identities but by product descriptions. A copper elbow, switch plate, hex nut, etc., are generic names for goods, and there is questionable value conferred on these items by issuing a brand identity. The term "Private Label" has been used extensively in recent literature and has become associated with the increasing options for distributors to purchase off-brands and label them with a store brand. In Figure 7-1, we examined the trend for distributors to private label products.

Figure 7-1 Distributor Interest in Private Labels

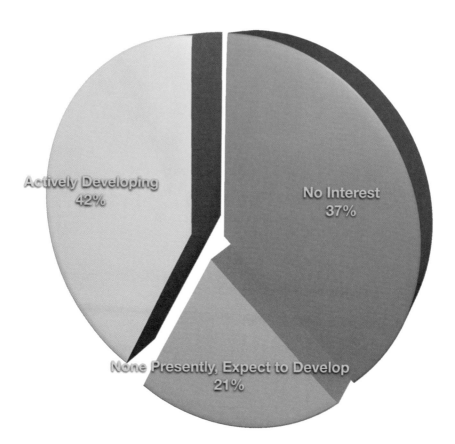

As seen in the figure:

- 37% had no interest in developing private labels
- 21% were not currently developing private labels, but were considering doing so
- 42% were actively developing private labels

Private labels can range from store brands to product-line brands to market brands. While private labeling strategies have been around since the beginning of distribution, the increased interest is primarily due to the influx of inexpensive off-brands from foreign shores.

A final category of brands and branding does not pertain to products, but to suppliers of different products. Names such as ORS Nasco, Matco-Norca, and Standard Products Inc., are associated with significant suppliers and importers of high-quality goods specific to a vertical market. For instance, ORS Nasco serves the industrial, PVF, and refinery markets and sells to distributors serving these markets. Standard Electric imports lighting and lighting fixtures and sells them to electrical and lighting distributors in Canada. Matco-Norca is a well known importer of plumbing valves and supplies to the North American plumbing wholesaler. These companies and many others serving specific vertical markets started out years ago as largely master distributors or importers. Master distributors carry C&D item inventory in bulk and offer place and time functions for these items in immediate-need situations. Master distributors often had to secure foreign brands as domestic brands with well-established channels didn't see or acknowledge their place and time value adds. Over time, the master distributors began to broaden their product portfolio and their global supplier base. Opportunities arose to add A&B item inventory and challenge domestic brands for distributor warehouse space. Today, organizations such as Standard Products Inc., Matco-Norca, and ORS Nasco have migrated well beyond their roots, becoming formidible suppliers to vertical industries and challenging domestic brands for leadership. We call these channel members "global master distributors" and while the moniker may not wholly describe their functions, these companies have significant advantages over traditional product manufacturers. These include the ability to source globally at the best cost/quality options, the ability to increase value added by quickly increasing the product portfolio, the ability to lower channel costs by lowering the number of transactions, and a speed-to-market that is often better than traditional manufacturers. These channel brands are known by the name of their company, and for all intents and purposes, the company and their functions *are* the brand. Global master distributors and their channel brands are successfully vying for and gaining share at the expense of domestic brands. Many of these companies have solid histories that stretch back decades, and their future is bright as evidenced by the insert supplied from an interview with David Nathaniel, CEO of Standard Products Inc., in Montreal, Quebec.

Standard Products Inc. started in Montreal, Quebec, in 1983. The company began as an importer of specialty lighting products to lighting stores, lighting distributors, and electrical distributors. The company secured the exclusive distribution rights to the Iwasaki (EYE) brand in Canada in 1988 and developed expertise in halogen and HID lamps. Other lines followed, and today the company secures items from all over the world, including (among others) China, Korea, Japan, U.S., Europe, India and Mexico. Today, the company has products in 15 separate functional categories and 6000 SKUs, including lighting for commercial, industrial, and institutional applications. Sales volume is not disclosed as the company is privately held. Estimates are that the company's volume puts it in the top 5% in sales for distribution entities in North America. The company has 150 full-time employees.

The company moved from a primary warehouse in Montreal to additional stocking locations in Toronto and Vancouver, covering over 175,000 square feet. In addition, the company has five sales offices across Canada and full e-commerce capabilities.

In the early years, Standard Products Inc. was a master distributor because it "didn't have enough volume to be a direct source." Over time, as sales grew, the company has become a "primary supplier of A, B, C, and D items." Many of the lines offer exclusives, and lines from outside North America are brought in through Vancouver or the St. Lawrence Seaway. While the company uses foreign agents as liaisons for product sources, these arrangements eventually move to a direct relationship with the vendor. Seventy percent of the products are Standard Products-branded, while approximately 30% are manufacturer brands. The product costs, innovation, and quality are "as good or better than GE, Phillips, Sylvania or other main line suppliers."

As the company's products grew, it began to wrap services around the products, including technical expertise in new and complex applications, special delivery options and channel services that lower transaction and holding costs for distributors, and manufacturing and assembly for select applications. The company also offers a full quality-control process, product development through marketing department and technicians, and code verification for products from their lab at the Montreal Facility.

Standard Products Inc. is a prime example of the ascension of global master distributors and channel brands. As channels globalize, we expect to see these entities dominate over traditional manufacturer direct brands.

Implications for Brand Strategies

We end this section with our estimate of changes in brand strategies for both the wholesaler and domestic manufacturer. In the past, brand development through distribution and for the larger companies has been an important part of the channel partnership. Today, many of the traditional marketing events are wasteful or simply lack impact, given the rise of off-brands. Figure 7-2 lists the traditional brand-based activities and how these have and will continue to change given the globalization of manufactured products.

Figure 7-2

Traditional Activity	Implications Arising From Increased Use of Off-Brands or Channel Brands
Co-Op Brand Domestic Advertising	Decrease in Overall Activity. Selective Product Advertising
Domestic Brand Sales Promotion	Decrease in Overall Activity. Most of Expenditures are Wasted as Products are Mature and Bought at Needed. Used by Domestic Brands For Capturing Share with Short Term Pricing and Incentives.
Domestic Brand Trade Advertising	Movement from Product and Technology Advertising to Promotion of Services and Ease of Doing Business.
Brand Awareness Campaigns and Sales Blitzes	Reduction in Domestic Brand Activity. PR Events are Highly Specialized. Channel Brands Increase Brand Building Activities Directed Toward Channel Services and End Users.
Marketing Organizations and Joint Marketing Programs for Domestic Brands	Channel Conflict Increases Between Traditional Cooperatives/Buying Groups/Marketing Organizations and Domestic Brands. Joint Planning Efforts Between Distributors and Domestic Brands is Greatly Reduced.

The far left column is labeled "Traditional Activity," and the right column lists "Implications" or changes in traditional branding strategies. Currently, much of distribution relies on manufacturer co-op dollar funding for marketing events. The basic format is dollar matching, in which the distributor spends a dollar, and the manufacturer matches it. Co-op budgets for major suppliers can swell into the tens of thousands of dollars per distributor and involve numerous marketing events. Most off-brands don't offer co-op funding, and most respondents from our survey don't seem to mind. We believe that many manufacturers are stuck in a cycle of providing co-op funds to their distribution base without careful scrutiny of how these funds are used or if they are entirely effective. In our experience, distributors, don't always adequately measure the effect of co-op expenditures. They conduct many confusing marketing activities without financially valid marketing. The upshot of inadequate financial measures and traditional approaches to co-op dollars is that they will, at least in prudent companies, be pared back or financially justified before usage. We don't see off-brand suppliers upping their co-op budgets, and they can be an albatross around the necks of domestic brands that don't verify their effectiveness.

Sales promotion is defined as a short-term incentive to buy. These include numerous pricing programs, such as the baker's dozen (buy 12, get one free), sales spiffs, and trip incentives for sales performance. Sales promotions are tactical and not strategic, but they often dominate marketing events for domestic brands and buying groups. Much like co-op expenditures, sales promotion is largely overdone and not scrutinized for effectiveness. In the flat world where information is instantaneous, the attractiveness of a lower price for inventory loading programs is fairly low. Hence, we believe sales promotion, like co-op usage, will decrease. Off-brands don't offer these supporting programs but, again, they don't have to. They deal with an average price decrease of 35% and EDLP (everyday low price).

Trade advertising for domestic brands has been reduced in many business markets. This is due both to a consolidation of manufacturers and recognition that, in mature markets, advertising to the distribution base should be very selective. Much of the advertising that is done for distribution involves new technologies, product features, and unique channel services provided by vendor(s). Brand advertising for established products is rare unless the manufacturer is going after new markets with existing technologies. Hence, we expect general advertising for domestic brands to remain very selective. Conversely, we expect advertising on channel services, new technologies, and channel brand suppliers to remain strong.

Public relations campaigns for industrial companies are increasingly rare. We have seen them used to build awareness for technical or service superiority, code compliance, and recovering from product recalls, worker strikes, or financial turnarounds. While public relations work has its place, it will become increasingly rare in mature industrial markets. Channel brands are active in using public relations events to develop market awareness of their services. This is one of the few places where public relations work is growing in industrial channels.

Joint market planning between manufacturer and vendor was, in past decades, a given for growing share through independent distribution. According to past logic, distributors were "partners" in the manufacturer's effort to grow market share.[1] With the introduction of off-brands and globalization of manufacturing, however, many manufacturers can consider themselves fortunate if their partners don't turn into competitors. Joint planning and partnership work, while valid for new technologies or complex products, don't make sense when the manufacturer is facing competition from off-brands, particularly when it adds cost to the whole value chain. Thus, we see a decrease in these efforts and relegation of the partnership talk to a time when domestic brands dominated domestic markets.

The decline of domestic brands and brand building activities is an outcome of the product pricing disparity between domestic suppliers and off-brands. It is enhanced by the flat world where global low pricing can be checked 24/7. There are few bright spots for marketing communications departments and channel service providers who have depended on brand building activities and advertising and co-op budgets of domestic manufacturers. Channel brand suppliers and service providers of information technology are a few of those areas where brand activities are valid and valuable. Much of the co-op spending, sales promotion, and partnering stressed in prior decades simply is not value added today. Buying groups that seek marketing funds from vendors and trumpet channel building activities in the form of marketing events may not be helping their members. It makes little sense to develop programs and promotions for products that are significantly outgunned by price in a thin margin business. As such, we expect the mission and market-ing event focus of buying groups to change.

---

[1] Anderson, J and Narus, J., "Turn Your Industrial Distributors Into Partners," March 1986, *Harvard Business Review Reprints.*

CHAPTER eight

Channel Costs in Decline:
Manufacturing and Cowboy Economics

We had the opportunity to present a preliminary analysis of this survey at a joint distributor/manufacturer conference attended by firms in a single industry. The distributors greeted the message with receptivity and thought. The comments from the manufacturers can be best described as denial. Scepticism and wariness in the face of significant, disruptive change is understandable but counterproductive. Denial only makes the problem worse since it delays action. Manufacturers that serve these industries and face the volume and rapidity of change have reason for concern. The familiar and tested strategies of the past are becoming irrelevant. Organizational change theorists tell us that organizations and people change when the fear of not changing is greater than the fear of changing. We hope that the preceding sections have instilled a healthy fear of the status quo. We will attempt, in the material that follows, to reduce the fear of the future by demystifying the changes that are occurring and analyzing prospective strategies with which manufacturers can meet these challenges. If we can reduce the stasis momentum that causes organizations to stagnate in the face of changing environments and replace it with change momentum, our purposes will have been achieved. To provide a historical perspective for our recommendations, we trace the history of livestock channels over the 90 year period from 1860 to 1950 and demonstrate how technology reduces costs in distribution systems while increasing quality.

The Cowboy Gets "Flattened"

Dramatic changes, indeed upheavals, in markets and industries are rarely the result of isolated changes in practices or economics. Almost universally, they are the result of a confluence or "perfect storm" of events that occur, if not simultaneously, then in close temporal juxtaposition. Rarely is any one event enough to cause the cataclysmic changes that occur in industries. A combination of events is more than sufficient. As we noted in *Cowboy Economics,* a cherished piece of American history—the fabled cattle drives of the 1800s—offers an interesting insight into this process and, indeed, into the changing "cowboy economics" of today's durable goods supply chain. The most legendary of the drives, which traveled up the Chisholm Trail through Central Texas to the railhead at Abilene, Kansas, began in earnest in 1866[1] as cattle ranchers sought to profit from the higher beef prices available at the slaughterhouses of Omaha and Chicago. Professional drovers, the logistics and distribution experts of the time, would contract with ranchers to drive the cattle to the railhead. A typical drive might include as many as 3,000 head of cattle, 10 to 15 trail-hands, a cook, trail boss, chuck wagon and supplies. It would require six weeks to complete as the cattle grazed their way north to the railroad.[2] While highly romanticized, this inward supply chain as we would call it today was labor intensive, sometimes dangerous, and conferred little value-added to the merchandise, the cattle. Stampedes, lightning storms, and dangerous river crossings all required the tender loving care of the cowboys—replete with whoops, lassos, and cutting horses—just to maintain the merchandise in salable condition. Not surprisingly, this high cost, slow, low valued-added supply chain was soon eliminated when a better alternative became available. Cattle drives only lasted for some twenty years, fading into history as the railroads pushed into Texas.

Several other events occurring in rapid succession served to simplify this long distance supply chain and reduce non-value added effort. Communication between vendor and purchaser was greatly enhanced by the telegraph. Western Union's initial transcontinental line was completed in 1861, and telegraph services grew rapidly throughout the country thereafter, boosted in part by the hundreds of miles of telegraph cable strung during the Civil War. By 1866, Western Union had 75,686 miles of wire and operated some 2,250 telegraph offices.[3] Suddenly, commercial communications between vendor and purchaser were instantaneous. Purchase orders, acknowledgments, and receipts could all be exchanged without regard for distance. Concurrently, there was a change in producers due to technology. Barbed wire was produced by Joseph Glidden, a 60-year-old from DeKalb, Illinois, in 1874. Barbed wire put an end to free grazers who let their livestock graze unimpeded over the available land. Barbed wire allowed ranchers to fence off their spreads and, as such, there were powerful ranch "brands" and a sudden disappearance of free grazers.

Despite the progress in logistics and communication, the supply chain between the ranch and the table still embodied a wealth of inefficiencies. Live cattle were still shipped, albeit by railroad, to slaughterhouses located near the centers of consumption.

Railroads maintained a host of facilities intended to care for live cattle as they made their way to the major population centers to be slaughtered, butchered, and consumed. The advent of the refrigerated rail car in about 1870[4] allowed the meat packing industry to move closer to the original source of supply. Gustavus Swift of Chicago cut blocks of ice from Lake Michigan, put them in insulated rail cars, and competed with the local butchers in population centers in the Northeast with precut, "embalmed" beef. Soon thereafter, with the help of ammonia-based refrigerants and local ice plants, meat packing centers grew in such western locales as Chicago, St. Paul, Omaha, Sioux City, St. Louis, Kansas City, Denver, Oklahoma City, and Fort Worth. Once it became possible to ship refrigerated carcasses to the population centers where consumers lived, it was no longer necessary to ship all the non-consumable parts of the cattle on the hoof or to create facilities for the cattle. Again, non-value added elements of the supply chain had been eliminated, and the movement of goods from producer to consumer had been accelerated while cost was reduced. This process has continued until today some 90 percent of the beef consumed is "boxed beef"—that is, wholesale cuts of beef, vacuum-packed and refrigerated for transport to the retailer where it is butchered into retail cuts.[5]

The final developments in this convergence was the implementation of beef grading standards by the U.S. Department of Agriculture in 1925,[6] the automation of grain fed beef by the 1950s, and refrigerated trucking by the 1940s. With the advent of these technologies, the chain of long distance supply and purchase of beef products was complete. Wholesalers could order beef and receive acknowledgment of their orders instantaneously by telegraph (and shortly thereafter via telephone). They could specify the quality required according to a standardized classification system, and they could receive the butchered meat quickly by refrigerated shipment. Livestock could be fed, raised, and rendered without significant movement, and the stockyards in Cincinnati and Chicago disappeared. Much of the waste and non-value-added activity had been eliminated from the system, and the cowboy, the rancher, the stockyard, and great slaughterhouses were obsolete. The world of beef distribution got flat. A conjunction of technological events dramatically reduced the significance of place, time, and distance and allowed vast amounts of waste in the value stream to be eliminated. Sadly, perhaps, a host of jobs dedicated to the movement of live cattle to the point of consumption were eliminated as well. The cowboy was "outsourced" as railway men, refrigeration technicians, telegraphers, and the like squeezed him out of the value stream.

What Happened?

To understand what happened to yesterday's cowboy and, indeed, what today's hard-goods manufacturers and their distributor partners are going through, we must begin by understanding the forces that are changing the competitive landscape.

Porter's[7] model holds that the degree of industry rivalry—the competitive intensity—is the function of five primary forces:

- The ease with which new competitors can enter the market.
- The level of power concentrated in buyers. In this case, the degree of channel power held by distributors and users as opposed to that held by manufacturers.
- The availability of substitute products and services. These are not mere like-for-like replacements, but are new classes of products and technology that can be substituted. For example, the manufacturer of laser drilling equipment may find itself threatened by newly cost-competitive water-jet drilling equipment. Downloading movies and cable movies-on-demand are substitutes for video rental shops.
- The bargaining power of suppliers. Small manufacturers of air conditioning and refrigeration equipment may find themselves at the mercy of large, corporate-owned manufacturers of compressors and fan motors.
- The degree of rivalry among existing firms. A competitive situation in which several manufacturers are vying for the attention of a limited number of distributors in a given channel is more competitive than it would be if only one manufacturer were present.[7]

We will examine each of these forces, paying particular attention to those that are most affected by the new realities of globalization.

New Entrants

First, and arguably most obvious, the threat of new entrants has been dramatically enhanced by the communications and logistics revolutions. Most apparent is the ease with which offshore competitors can access formerly proprietary distribution channels. Websites, browser technologies, and online directories and aggregators such as Alibaba.com have granted suppliers around the world immediate access to U.S. distribution. Alibaba.com, named "Best of the Web" seven years running by *Forbes Magazine*, offers a convenient virtual marketplace, complete with video conferencing and instant messaging. Suppliers and purchasers can meet virtually and in real time to discuss product specifications, delivery, price, and payment terms for hundreds of thousands of products. Suppliers can, of course, post their catalog, while buyers can post their needs to permit searching and bidding by prospective suppliers worldwide. The flattening of the world has removed all the former barriers that kept suppliers from finding distributors and buyers from finding suppliers. Now they can connect regardless of physical distance between them. This peer-to-peer collaboration, or "crowdsourcing" as Don Tapscott and Anthony Williams christened it,[8] has enabled individual firms to deal with other individual firms throughout the world, regardless of their size. Globalization is no longer just for multinational corporations. Other resources, including Ariba Inc., China Manufacturing Network, and Buyers Bridge, serve as the industrial equivalents of Facebook, introducing vendors and customers without regard to location and distance. This same electronic wizardry, along with the logistics prowess available through UPS, FedEx, and others have also served to drastically reduce or even eliminate the costs of switching suppliers.

Two traditional product differentiators that have historically inhibited the entry of new competitors are rapidly losing their effect in traditional hard goods channels. As we have noted, distributors and users both perceive little value in the brand identity of these industrial products. While branded products continue to be available only through the proprietary channels, distributors and users are not constrained to these channels when brand identity has lost its value.

Similarly, proprietary product specifications and industry certifications have lost much of their ability to restrict the entry of new competitors. Commoditized industrial goods are, by definition, nonproprietary. Ironically, industry standards, quality registrations, and safety certifications, once thought to be useful in keeping lower-cost offshore competition at bay, are now being used by these very competitors to reassure long-distance buyers of the quality and suitability of the products. Just as the USDA beef grading standards allowed the sight-unseen purchase of beef carcasses in our cowboy parable, UL, CE, SAE, ISO, ASTM, and similar standards allow today's distributor purchasing managers to buy through long distance arrangements with, if not complete, at least reasonable confidence. Similarly, these standards provide a level of comfort to users who feel more comfortable foregoing familiar brands if the offshore goods they are purchasing comply with universally known and accepted standards.

Finally, the cost (or at least the price) advantage possessed by these offshore entities simply facilitates their entry into the market. The average 30% price advantage enjoyed by these newcomers is more than enough impetus for domestic distributors and users to try them. Indeed, this price advantage is used by these new entrants to garner sufficient initial interest among domestic buyers.

Buyer Channel Power

Nothing has served to redistribute channel power like the flattening of the world of durable goods. Buyers at both the distributor and user levels now have perfect information. Details of the worldwide availability of products, their prices, anticipated delivery times, technical specifications, and virtually any other data are now available with a few keystrokes and mouseclicks.

Declining brand equity, as documented by this survey, also reduces the power of the manufacturer and increases that of the distributor and buyer. When the equity of the brand is high, and it is available only through the authorized channel, distributors and users are loathe to seek alternative suppliers. As brand equity declines, and satisfactory alternatives become readily available, particularly at attractive prices and with little effort, switching begins in earnest and manufacturers lose their power to influence channel partners.

Finally, the profits of channel partners, particularly those of distributors in a manufacturer-distributor chain, are critical determinants of partner loyalty and manufacturer channel power. Distributors whose profits are squeezed by the high costs associated with branded products as compared to off-brand, offshore substitutes will be the ones whose loyalty fades most quickly. Manufacturers whose practices have been aimed at maintaining price premiums through the addition of questionable "value added" services, will be the first to lose channel power as their channel partners defect to alternatives in an effort to protect their margins. Those that have used high prices in the channel to offset a failure to be cost-competitive or to cross-subsidize low margin, high volume OEM business will be the most vulnerable. Without major cost reduction work, they will have the least freedom to react to the threat of reduced channel power and channel partner loyalty without unacceptable reductions in both the top and bottom lines of their income statements.

When distributors seek alternative, offshore suppliers and accept the responsibility of offshore procurement and logistics, they may be seen to be backward integrating and moving up the supply chain. They are reducing their role as channel partners and becoming, in effect, competitors to the domestic manufacturer. In years past, the difficulties inherent in assuming this role were considerable, and only the largest, most sophisticated distributors could entertain such a move. As we have seen, the ease with which offshore suppliers can now be found has enabled many smaller, less well-capitalized distributors to adopt this strategy. As they do, channel power continues its flight from manufacturer to distributor.

An important though tangential issue is that of distributor areas of primary responsibility, or whatever euphemistic name is given to distributor territories to circumvent antitrust laws. It should be painfully obvious by now that the same confluence of technology and logistics capability that permits distributors to source offshore products with unprecedented ease will allow users anywhere to source from whomever they wish. Conversely, the ease with which e-commerce storefronts can be established enables distributors to sell to anyone they please, regardless of location. Attempts to control the efforts of distributors and to constrain their sales to authorized areas are now a legacy of an earlier time. They rarely worked well in the past and, in most cases, will not work at all now. The one possible exception to this rule occurs when on-site warranty service obligations exist. This is a distinct exception for most of the commoditized, easily transported industrial goods under consideration here.

Finally, the efforts of joint market planning and "partnering" with distributors by branded manufacturers are largely anachronistic. When brands were recognized and dominant, the manufacturer could work with the distributor to grow share versus competitive manufacturers. With the decline of brand power and explosion in global off-brands, excessive joint planning or "partnering" activities are not valued and redundant. It simply makes no sense to conduct expensive marketing events and planning for products that are mature and largely differentiated by price.

Supplier Bargaining Power

Although not immediately obvious, the OEM's suppliers or potential suppliers have a role to play here as well. Offshore suppliers, perhaps those that were recruited by domestic manufacturers as they undertook their own outsourcing activities, can now locate distributors and users of their products with unprecedented ease. Domestic manufacturers of branded products that have developed offshore suppliers to reduce costs, but captured most or all of the resulting savings to bolster their own flagging profitability or to cross-subsidize low margin sales, are the most vulnerable to this. While noncompete clauses may have been included in the supply agreements with offshore suppliers, we wish you the best of luck in enforcing them. In any case, the elaborate network of family-owned companies that is the rule in China for example, can easily circumvent these obligations. Once they become aware of the marketplace price of their products at the manufacturer to distributor level, these offshore suppliers will have a powerful incentive to circumvent the domestic manufacturer. Distributors, of course, will have an equally strong incentive to bypass the domestic manufacturer of branded products and purchase directly from the offshore source. Given the laxity of intellectual property enforcement in many of the areas from which these products are sourced, they may find their way to distributor shelves complete with counterfeit trademarks. Manufacturers and trademark owners can, of course, prevail upon their distributors to prevent this from occurring. When they do so, however, they create their own unpleasant version of Sophie's choice—the classic dilemma between two terrible choices. If they react, they further weaken the value of the trademark and may cause the distributor to opt for private label products. If they don't react, they risk losing their trademark through lack of enforcement.

Preexisting Manufacturer Rivalry

The number of preexisting domestic manufacturers has an important bearing on the competitive landscape facing these manufacturers as they respond to the globalized world of distribution. When multiple domestic suppliers court the distribution channel, distributor loyalty is likely to be low and the propensity to switch between them great. This only exacerbates the problems created by the ready availability of low-priced offshore competition. The presence of multiple competitors offering similar if not essentially identical products has, in all likelihood, reduced the value of brand identity in the collective minds of both the distributors and their customers. This reduced brand equity and the readiness to switch between suppliers has probably reduced the potential for differentiation and made price the overwhelming, if not sole, competitive factor. The increased importance of price provides an additional incentive to switch to offshore, off-brand suppliers, given the large savings available.

The Sum of the Parts

Ironically, it is the increasing sophistication of communications technology and logistics expertise that has simplified the activities of the distribution channel to the point that traditional manufacturer-distributor relationships are fading. The ease with which global buyers and sellers can find and communicate with each other, the ready availability of logistics expertise from trusted suppliers, the ease with which distributors can switch sources of supply, the declining importance of brand identity, the widespread conformance to international product standards, and, of course, the dramatic cost reductions to be realized through offshore sourcing, have all come together to create the perfect storm for traditional domestic manufacturers of branded industrial products. This perfect storm will drive fundamental strategic changes for those manufacturers willing and able to respond to the challenges. It will drive failure and retrenchment at those unwilling to undertake a wholesale reexamination of their distribution channel business. In the next sections, we turn our attention to the tools and thought processes necessary to undertake this reexamination.

¹ Ramos, M.G. 1990, Texas Almanac http://www.texasalmanac.com/history/highlights/cattle/

² Skaggs, J., The Handbook of Texas Online University of Texas at Austin. http://www.tsha.utexas.edu/handbook/online/articles/CC/.html

³ Cornell, W., Glover, J., 1941, The Development of American Industries, Their Economic Significance. Prentice Hall, New York.

⁴ Ibid.

⁵ Epley, R., University of Minnesota Extension http://www.extension.umn.edu/distribution/nutrition/DJ5968.html

⁶ Harris, J., Cross, H., and Savell, J, History of Meat Grading in the United States, Texas A&M University; http://meat.tamu.edu/history.html

⁷ Porter, M. (1985). *Competitive Advantage: Creating and Sustaining Superior Performance.* New York: The Free Press.

⁸ Tapscott, D. and Williams, A. (2006), *Wikinomics: How Mass Collaboration Changes Everything.* New York: Penguin Books.

CHAPTER nine

Mega-Changes in the Distributor's Structure and Channel Relationships

We have salted the text with changes in the operational and marketing strategy of distributors in the globalized or "flat" world. There is little that will be left unchanged due to globalization, but the events in this chapter are the most prominent and are currently underway. These changes are gradual for the most part, but can have a tidal-wave effect over time. Some are full paradigm shifts. The events may not yet have appeared in a specific vertical market, but they are prominent in many of them. The changes can involve entire functional areas, established channel relationships, and change the financial management and cost structure of the distributor or channel. As an overview of the more notable changes, we have included Figure 9-1, which gives the change event, its definition, and implications for change.

Figure 9-1

Event Number	Change	Definition	Implications
1	Profit Dollar Shift	Decrease in Margin Dollars Due to Lower Cost of Goods Base	Distributors May Not be Able to Offset Margin Dollar Reduction With Increase in Sales. Reduction in Support Expenses Will Follow.
2	Purchasing Systems	Vendor Base Changes From Domestic Brands	Distributor Vendors Include Master Distributors, Alliances, Foreign Direct Sellers and Importers. Domestic Brand Relationships May be In Jeopardy
3	Purchasing Processes	Foreign Sources Require Different Purchasing Skills	Dealing With Foreign Suppliers Requires New Skill Sets and Activities Including Product Testing, Liability Insurance Sourcing, Expanded Logistics, and Currency Management
4	Cooperative and Buying Group Schism	Channel Conflict Between Domestic Brands and Cooperatives and Buying Groups	Cooperative Advertising Dollars from Domestic Vendors May Decrease. Relationships Become Strained as cooperatives Become Importers.
5	Sales Promotion Efforts Decline	Sales Promotion and Marketing Efforts with Domestic Vendors Decline	Additional Channel Conflict With Domestic Vendors as Low Price Wins Over Sales Promotion
6	Special Pricing Agreements	Off-Sheet Pricing to Meet Competitive Situations	SPA's or Special Pricing Agreements are Deemed Wasteful by Distributors. Foreign Vendors Offer "EDLP" - Everyday Low Prices.

As seen in the figure, there are six main change events under the column heading "Event Number." The "Change Event" title is given in the next column followed by its "Definition" and "Implications." For example, the first change event is "Profit Dollar Shift."It is defined as the decrease in margin dollars from purchasing off-brands. The implications include managing for a possible significant drop in margin dollars. We use Figure 9-1 as a guideline for the remainder of this chapter.

Profit Dollar Shift

As mentioned in Chapter 2, Figure 2-4, the typical distributor cannot afford to forego the pricing advantage of off-brands. In the figure, various levels of purchases were given, along with their effect on net income from off-brands. Figure 2-4 was decidedly short-term, and it illustrated the short-term profit potential and market necessity of buying products that cost, on average, 35% less than domestic brands. Over time, however, the total margin dollars that distributors deal with may fall significantly. Consider a $100 million distributor who nets a 25% margin on domestic products, and cost of goods are $75 million. If 100% of the domestic inventory were replaced by off-brands at a 35% cost reduction, the distributor's margin dollars, assuming a 25% margin, would fall to $16.25 million. In essence, there would be approximately $9 million less in operating dollars for the distributor to work with. Of course, it is improbable that 100% of demand can be filled by off-brands at a cost of 35% less than existing brands. However, there will be a significant amount of margin dollars lost due to a lower cost of goods. In the short run, the distributor that is first with foreign brands may capture some share with a lower market price, but in the long run, we believe most distributors will have access to off-brands at lower prices, and the market price will reach equilibrium at price points that are reflective of the cost reduction to the distribution base. Since industrial markets grow at the rate of GDP of 2.5%, there will not be top-line sales growth that can fund the loss of margin dollars from off-brands. In short, we see significant adjustments to the operating platform for most distributors, and our best guess follows.

In our 2006 release, *Restructuring the Distribution Sales Effort*,[1] we cited research from end users about the need for cost reduction in distributor sales forces. Many end users would rather have a price decrease equal to the historic channel cost of distributor sales forces than traditional solicitation frequencies provided by the distribution base. The reason for this is complex, but it has to do with poor sales allocation methods by distributors and the maturation of products that need less sales support. Our long-term forecast is for a gradual reduction in outside and inside solicitation efforts from distributors. Currently, global commodity inflation has masked the need for solicitation cost reduction. However, as commodity prices fall, and off-brands become prevalent, the need for cost reduction in solicitation efforts will resurface.

Service management, which includes costs to serve, service allocation, and service process improvement, will reappear as firms struggle with growth resulting from consolidation. Today, consolidation represents the primary mode of growth for distributors, and Greenfield sites have largely disappeared as a means of growing the firm. Merchant wholesaling is still dominated by small firms, and many, nearing the third generation, are candidates for acquisition. In recent years, service management has fallen out of fashion as labor costs have been contained. Labor costs will remain low for a few years until global labor pools begin to tighten and pressure on wages rises.[2] As commodity prices fall and labor costs increase, the need to contain service costs will rise accordingly. For all practical purposes, labor costs represent 65% to 75% of the typical wholesaler's operating expenses. Most wholesalers don't have sophisticated means to evaluate services, and this will need to change. The ability to measure service quality, improve processes while taking error and cost out, and aligning services with customers who can afford them are subjects that will increasingly gain interest. And a vital part of service measurement and management is activity costing and activity management, which we believe will gain increased acceptance among wholesalers. Activity management has been used in distribution for close to two decades. However, initial efforts were cumbersome, and there were glaring problems in assumptions with capacity and activity drivers incorporating fallacious logic. We believe activity based costing and management will undergo a renaissance, moving away from traditional accounting driven analyses to more scientifically based statistical analyses of greater value to operating managers.

Purchasing Systems

Purchasing systems are defined as the channel relationships required to move a product from the manufacturer to the distributor. They include entities that take title to the goods, as well as entrants who facilitate the flow of goods. For off-brands, the purchasing system has become increasingly crowded, as any number of firms are available to help with the sourcing of offshore goods. Figure 9-2 lists six common sources of off-brands, along with their value added to the distributor.

Figure 9-2

Off-Brand Source	Modus Operandi/Comments
Name Brand Manufacturer	Typically Last to Offer Off-Brands For Fear of Cannibalizing Existing Brands. Can be Formidable Supplier if Pricing is Competitive and Parent Organization Doesn't Overburden with Corporate Overhead.
Short Line Manufacturer	A Solid Competitive Move to Offer Products That Aren't in Current Mix But You Have the Channel Relationships to Source. Look for Partial Investment in offshore Manufacturing as a Signal of Staying Power.
Direct from Off-Brand Supplier	Best Product Price Deal for Distributor. Difficulty in Inventory Balancing and Management Unless Volume is Significant. Distributor Needs Solid Procurement. Quality Validation and Insurance
Master Distributor	Best Sourcing Option For Channel Services of Inventory, Pricing, and Exemption from Internal Procurement Hassles. Best Option for Smaller Distributors Who Can't Build Sufficient Volume.
Importer	A New Model, Like a Master Distributor, but Doesn't Inventory or Always Take Title. Importers Can Develop Relationships, Aggregate Orders to Reduce Transport Costs and Establish Product Standards and Testing. Watch for Growth of this Model, Typically Specific to Vertical Markets.
Cooperative/Alliance	A Powerful Model for Distributors Who Work Together to Maximize Volume and Agree on Product and Service Platform. Can be Unhinged by Distributors Who Grow Large and Can Go it Alone. Also Has Significant Conflicts with Existing Branded Manufacturer Relationships.

We have found all six of these entrants in many of the vertical markets within durable goods distribution. Our purpose is to introduce them to the reader as potential partners in the global economy.

Name-brand manufacturers can be reliable suppliers of off-brands. While we have defined off-brands as non-domestic brands, many domestic suppliers have chosen to develop off-brands in hopes of stemming share-loss of their well known domestic brands. The advantage of buying an off-brand from a domestic supplier is that the wholesaler has an established relationship with the supplier, and the issues of meeting code requirements and certifications and having adequate protection against product liability suits are few. The problem in dealing with off-brands manufactured by domestic companies is that the parent companies typically have the cost burdens earlier identified in the research, including expensive stateside management and product development and shareholder demands for superior returns. In the long run, it is difficult for us to rationalize how domestic companies will overcome cost disadvantages in mature markets unless they thoroughly attack cost overages, which are predominantly the management, research and development, and excess costs found in North American operations.

Short-line manufacturers can be credible sources for distributors for securing off-brands. A short-line manufacturing example would be a manufacturer of tubs and showers that allies with an offshore manufacturer of water closets and lavatories and sells the fixtures along with their line of tubs and showers. The advantages to this type of arrangement are many. First, the short-line manufacturer doesn't have a historical bias aimed at protecting the domestic prices of an existing line. The line they "manufacture" comes from a strategic alliance with an outside manufacturer, and there is not an inherent disposition to "protect" the leading brand. Short-line manufacturers also have the advantages of knowing the domestic distribution channel, familiarity with codes and certifications, and adequate coverage against product liability suits. Many wholesalers are finding short-line manufacturers to be a valuable source for off-brands, and we expect this part of the channel to grow.

A growing part of purchases are from direct relationships with off-brand suppliers. In the initial stages of globalization, some two decades ago, the risks from off-brand products were high and included the risk of counterfeiting, product liability and return/warranty risk. As offshore manufacturers gained experience in dealing with North American markets and intermediaries like global master distributors, many of these risks have abated. This is especially true if the foreign entity has worked as a contract or licensed manufacturer(s) for established domestic manufacturers. Typically, the best purchase price is to be gained from dealing with foreign manufacturers, but there must also be adequate precautions when taking this route. There are any number of agents, testing facilities, and insurance companies that can mitigate risk when dealing directly with foreign suppliers. We encourage distributors to carefully research these options when dealing with direct relationships. From our interviews, there are many large distribution companies that have set up in-house purchasing functions in Hong Kong, Shanghai, and Eastern Europe.

Master distributors, or more appropriately "global master distributors," have been mentioned in detail earlier in the text. There are numerous global master distributors serving merchant wholesaler-distributors, and they are generally aligned with a vertical industry. Most global master distributors have approved product sources, adequate insurance coverage for product liability, and well-established relationships with foreign suppliers. They are a good source for immediate-need items and act as regular replenishment vendors of stocked items. For those who cannot order container or partial container volume, global master distributors can offer a competitive price for smaller shipments of off-brands.

Importers represent a new channel entrant covering off-brands. They differ from direct relationships and agents in that they often do not take title to goods. They work with competing manufacturers and offer stateside aggregation and short-term storage for off-brands. In our work, we see importers that succeed by working with new wholesalers and manufacturers. By having a variety of customers and vendors, they are able to offer container pricing while not necessarily requiring a container purchase. In several instances, we found importers who offered pricing that was equal to or better than what a distributor could get in a direct relationship when shipping partial containers. They do this by working with numerous wholesalers and driving volume discounts to the off-brand supplier. Because of the relative novelty of importers, we caution distributors to be thorough in understanding their code compliance, testing, product liability coverage, and processes to guard against counterfeit products.

There are also numerous informal alliances, cooperatives, and buying groups who are working with off-brands, either on a direct basis or through the previously mentioned sources. We have noticed sophisticated buying group efforts in the Jan-San, plumbing, automotive, and electronic sectors. Often, when a cooperative or buying group initiates a relationship with off-brand suppliers, there is significant channel conflict with domestic vendors. In some instances, cooperatives and buying groups will develop house brands for their membership, which are sourced primarily from overseas. The willingness of these existing channel entrants to come in conflict with domestic suppliers speaks to the needs of wholesalers and the attractiveness of off-brands.

Along with the various channel suppliers of off-brands, there are services that take the risk out of overbuying or buying the wrong inventory. These services are called "virtual inventory-sharing services" and include a variety of options for distributors to balance or shed slow-moving or obsolete inventory. These services exist because of the Internet and technology that allows a community of like distributors to post and trade off slow-moving, specialized, or wrongly purchased inventory. They offer considerable advantages in allowing distributors to close critical backorders by leveraging the inventory that exists on the shelves of similar distributors.

One such example is Warehouse TWO (www.warehousetwo. com) which is an inventory listing and clearance service for defined communities including: high purity fittings and valves, fluid power and process instrumentation. The service, started by Mark Tomalonis, offers distributors the chance to list slow-moving or obsolete inventory on the Warehouse TWO website. According to Tomalonis, "The service makes sense for any distribution vertical when any two of the following conditions exist:

- Product line has numerous parts numbers, and stocking the entire line by any one distributor is financially prohibitive
- Product line is highly configurable, and no one distributor can afford to stock all permutations
- Manufacturers choose to have little in the way of finished goods in stock, and lead times are longer than customers are willing to wait for
- The manufacturer has finished goods, but the only way for distributors to know what's in the factory stock is to call, e-mail, or fax for availability
- There exists a clearly defined and dominant manufacturer parts numbering system

The advantages for the service are numerous for both distributor and manufacturer. The distributor can offer a quick search service for customers and offer "heroic" recoveries for backordered or out of stock items. The manufacturer can often stock less finished goods and receives fewer requests from distributors to return inventory.

The service charges a posting fee for items that have a common nomenclature and are typically part of a manufacturer/distributor franchise or specific industry. There are four basic options for posting.

The charges for the service range from free to $200 per month. There is no fee for purchasing and only a fee for listing. Interested buyers simply contact sellers through the service and make their own arrangements to buy. To date, Warehouse TWO has over 60 manufacturers, 100 distributors in the community, and over 40,000 SKUs. The service is even listed as a value-added service on manufacturer sites. Finally, the financial returns for distributors are impressive, with reports of distribution entities selling over $50,000 in otherwise dead inventory at double-digit margins.

Warehouse TWO is an example of the effects of technology on established channels. Where inventory risk was high in the world before the Internet, the use of e-commerce and websites has allowed inventory-sharing services to flourish in many vertical markets. As such, the risk of overbuying or having obsolete inventory is greatly reduced by information sharing within a defined product/market community.

Purchasing Processes

The majority of purchasing management, software, and processes for the North American distributor have been arranged around domestic brands. Inclusive in these processes are economic order quantities, forecasts, volume price breaks, and domestic shipping times that determine the reorder points and reorder quantities for purchasing agents. Also, the financial value of relationships for domestic vendors include other non-initial cost factors, such as quality, reliability, insurance coverage, testing certifications, volume rebate dollars, and co-op dollars. For off-brands, the experience gained with domestic brands is typically not sufficient for purchasing agents and the associated management of cost of goods and assets. In essence, when buying off-brands, much changes, and new variables are introduced into the equation. Below, we have listed common changes to purchasing systems that are encountered while buying off-brands:

- Economic order quantities (EOQs) change due to differences in average inventory, container costs versus less-than-container costs, and costs per unit of inventory. In many instances, EOQs may not be applicable for off-brands.
- Return and warranty privileges can differ with off-brands.
- Quality and testing and application certifications can differ or should be researched with off-brands.
- Insurance coverage for product liability may not be sufficient from off-brand suppliers.
- Exchange rates may fluctuate, and purchasing agents and financial managers may need to learn to review currency forecasts or use exchange hedge instruments.

Purchasing agents should develop relationships with global master distributors, importers, short-line manufacturers, and inventory-sharing services that can perform some of the new channel functions and take risk out of the global supply chain.

Our experience in dealing directly with off-brand suppliers is that they prefer to ship container loads. However, for many distributors, container loads are not feasible and do not allow for sufficient balancing of inventory. When this is the case, partial containers are an option, but price typically increases 10% to 15%. There are also intermediaries or staging facilities in port cities that can combine orders for a full container in the country of origin. As the container is received stateside, the order is broken down into individual shipments. The order-cycle time lag in dealing with off-brands versus domestically manufactured brands can be substantial as can inventory costs. Hence, economic order quantities and reorder points and other inventory management tools typically need adjustment. Other "soft" factors, including certifications and warranty policies, should be thoroughly explored before dealing directly with an off-brand supplier.

A substantial concern is the product liability posed by purchasing an off-brand product. Unknown suppliers may not be properly insured or may not offer distributors coverage in a product liability lawsuit. A recent research project by Redmond, Ray and Gordon[3] found 11% of electrical contractors faced liability lawsuits for installed products, and slightly over 70% of the lawsuits are carried back to the distributor. For off-brands, a foreign manufacturer with no U.S. operations is "notoriously hard to serve with suit papers." The authors suggest, as defenses for the distributor, "enforceable indemnification and defense provision(s)" or listing under the manufacturer's policy as an "Additional Insured." In many instances, it may be prudent for the distributor to seek outside insurance to cover potential liability.[4] Our interviews found that any number of major insurers and their agents will underwrite product liability coverage. There is no standard policy available, and premiums can range between four, five or six figures. Terms are typically annual, but may be for two or three years. Finally, in the parlance of the insurers, distributors are encouraged to ask for the coverage trigger of an "occurrence" policy versus a "claims made" policy.

In our estimation, many distributors will rely on manufacturer policies and insurance to cover product liability. This, of course, is not recommended unless the distributor carefully checks the policies of the manufacturer. We would also recommend that the distributor hire a qualified product liability law firm to review manufacturer policies and procedures, as well as a qualified insurance agent to review coverage policies and offer advice for off-brands.

Product and testing certifications surfaced as a concern for distributor respondents. Underwriter's Laboratories in the electrical sector, ASTM and ASME in the plumbing and PVF sector, ASHRAE in air conditioning and refrigeration sector, and SAE in the automotive sector are all well known and respected testing standards and certifications organizations for product performance and safety. In our research, however, we found that many of these standards and certification firms had set up shop on foreign shores long ago. Many of the firms set up shop in China as they followed U.S. manufacturers overseas to provide their services for finished goods. Today, the firms service foreign manufacturers in developing standards for products sold in the country of manufacture. From our interviews with veteran distribution buyers of off-brands, we have yet to hear that certification and standards testing is an issue. However, when buying off-brands, we encourage distributors to compare the standards and certification on foreign products to domestic brands or brands that are scheduled to be displaced.

In closing the sections on purchasing systems and processes, we advise distributors to define, develop, and manage by a written process for off-brand purchases. The process would include previously mentioned elements of key alliances, product quality, product liability, purchasing system, purchasing metrics, and currency management steps. The process should specify control and feedback loops and position responsibility for each step. We have had the privilege of reviewing several processes for distributors who are seasoned in buying off-brands. Their purchasing processes were well documented and quite detailed. In one instance, the process was a multiple-step checklist of seven pages that included details on insurance, currency exchange rates, agents, and transport details from port to port to rail to drayage. Finally, we haven't spent much time on the subject of financial diligence in justifying the off-brand purchase. At the average pricing advantage of 35%, most off-brands with reasonable services and certifications are worth a try. However, we have seen disasters where distributors did not put pencil to paper when considering the full costs of off-brands, such as lowered turns, downpayments, and increased capital costs. In one instance, we found an engine parts distributor that was vying for off-brands at a cost advantage of 15%. The lowered turns, downpayments, and product problems were not modeled *prior* to the investment, and the distributor found the capital costs and inventory issues made the strategy financially unattractive.

Schism in Channel Relationships

The domestic brand has had a significant influence on existing channel relationships, and we expect that the cooperative or buying group will be in the thick of channel issues. Product development, advertising, sales promotion, and significant funding of industry associations and events is done by domestic brands through cooperatives. In turn, cooperatives and buying groups represent billions of purchases for domestic brands. However, because of the share loss of domestic vendors, much will change. As off-brands increase, there will be conflict arising from their purchases. Channel conflict, as in human conflict, is categorized by various stages of escalation (skirmish to shooting war) until relationships break off. Fortunately, most business relationships strive toward longevity, and the cessation of a working relationship is a last resort. There are, however, signs of stress in channel relationships, and we discuss them in the remainder of this section.

In industries where off-brands are recent developments, there is a propensity for domestic vendors to fund research on the issues of counterfeiting and product liability from off-brands. We have a jaundiced view of such research, as it often ends in scare-mongering and the deliberate frightening of the distribution base. In essence, the research is often biased from the start, and unless there are comparative statistics on the product liability claims of domestic brands versus off-brands, and historical reviews of similar events in like channels, etc., the research should be considered carefully. Included with the scare-mongering tactics are efforts by leading manufacturers to legislate barriers for off-brands. Typically, legislation is done around new certifications and testing standards is anti-import based, with claims of dumping or unfair advantages. Most of the time, legislative efforts fail—and in a spectacular fashion. As we have stressed throughout this text, the best chance for the domestic vendor is to determine where and how they can add value in the channel while competing on the global stage. Anything less than this will ultimately fail.

Some manufacturers will resort to strong-arm tactics, such as rescinding discounts and services or cessation of parts or all of product sales. This is especially true for smaller distributors that lack buying clout or channel power. However, smaller distributors are banding together through their cooperatives, buying groups, and informal alliances. In one instance, we found an alliance of 20 small and medium-size companies across North America that joined to bring off-brands to a central (Midwest) hub and redistribute them to alliance members. The result of their efforts over a course of years was financial security for them and bankruptcy for several domestic vendors. We caution powerful domestic vendors against fear tactics. Channel relationships have significant roots in human nature and emotion, and men learn to "hate the men they fear…"[5] In our experience, no amount of influence can salvage a channel relationship when a vendor has managed by fear and intimidation for an extended period.

Sales Promotion Decrease

Millions of dollars are spent by manufacturers on sales promotions with their distribution. These efforts are decidedly tactical in nature and use incentives to drive purchases in lieu of an out-and-out price war. Common promotions include trip programs, dollars-off programs, merchandise and cash incentives, and so forth. Most industrial markets are predicated on a demonstrable advantage in function and cost over the competition. Toward this goal, sales promotions can be effective in getting an end user to try an alternative product with the long-term goal being a switch in brand. However, as a tool to combat the significant price advantage of off-brands, sales promotion is a wasteful tactic. The research leads us to believe many distributors know this, but a significant amount do not. And there are plenty of cooperatives and marketing groups that stress sales promotion as evidence of value to the domestic vendor.

In the late 1970s and 1980s, the use of sales promotion in distributed markets was common. There were any number of seminars and courses on the subject and several books dedicated to distributors on the wisdom of using sales promotion. By the mid 1990s, which coincided with China's ascension in industrial manufacturing and NAFTA, we began to see a curtailment in sales promotion hype and logic. While many distributors have curtailed their expenditures in this area, others have continued the practice of intensive sales promotion. Through our consulting work, we have found much sales promotion to be counterproductive and not financially viable. Many companies have poorly defined goals and financial measures for understanding whether a particular promotion covered its investment. To help distributors in decision-making about a sales promotion program, we offer the following points:

- Use sales promotion where you have a technological or application advantage with a product or where you are switching brands. Don't consider a promotion that pits a domestic supplier, with few or no inherent advantages, against a market served by acceptable off-brands.
- Have a well-defined time period for the promotion.
- Develop a forecast of increased sales or margin dollars from the program and what sales volume is needed to cover the program's cost.
- Work toward cooperative funding (dollar for dollar) for the program.
- Train the sales force, both inside and outside, on the program.
- Monitor the program at defined time intervals; if it isn't succeeding, readjust or stop.

The conclusion to be drawn from the research and our experiences is that much of sales promotion is wasteful and unnecessary. Interestingly enough, off-brands are not offering much if any sales promotion, while domestic brands are keeping pace with historic levels of sales promotion and cooperative spending. The research suggests that the distribution base finds the attitude of domestic vendors profligate and of limited value versus the low-cost platform of off-brands.

Special Pricing Agreements

Many distributed markets use Special Pricing Agreements, or SPAs. Special Pricing Agreements are granted by manufacturers to give distributors a competitive price for a defined buying situation. Suppose that Distributor B sold Green Bay Widgets for $10 and was competing for the Rhinelander Job against Distributor M that sold Eau Claire widgets for $8.50. Distributor B would go to Green Bay Widgets and ask for a competitive price specific to the Rhinelander Job that would allow it to meet the competitive situation. This is called the "matching competition defense," and it is upheld under current U.S. pricing legislation.[6] The problem with the matching competition defense is twofold. First, the paperwork, filings, and follow-up is expensive and time-consuming. Second, there is, inherent in both the mechanism and a thin margin environment like distribution, an incentive to cheat.

Matching a price competition requires that both the distributor and manufacturer keep records of the special price, submit paperwork documenting when the special price was granted, when specially priced items were sold, and receipt of reimbursement for sales specific to the granted price. The paperwork is cumbersome and expensive and, depending upon whether the price was granted as a rebate on sales or a cost concession on a stock order, there could be carrying costs for excess specially priced inventory. Some associations have automated the process with EDI data sets. This has helped bring down the cost of the paperwork, but the process is still cumbersome.

Sometimes a special price is granted for a "phantom" situation. Suppose that Distributor F got an $8.50 price agreement on Green Bay Widgets and sold them to a Distributor B customer. Distributor B could complain to Green Bay Widgets and seek an injunction against the practice. But what if Distributor B did not know that the widgets Distributor F sold were Green Bay Widgets? What if the end buyer told Distributor B the widgets were not Green Bay Widgets but another brand? And, even if Distributor B found the widgets were of Green Bay manufacture and sought legal action, would they be able to trace the steps of the transaction(s) between Distributor F, Green Bay Widgets, and the end user? In a thin-margin, high-transaction environment where small price advantages on price-elastic commodities exist, the incentive to cheat is powerful and exacerbated by the difficulty of proof. Hence, we believe there is an inherent incentive to cheat when special pricing is available. Coincidentally, we believe that some manufacturers tolerate this and weigh the consequences of cheating versus the long-term gain attained by lowering price selectively in their markets.

Strategically, in the flat world where information is of nominal cost, product standards well-known, and a gaping price differential exists in identical goods, the special pricing mechanism is a bust. Economically, distributor buyers will not seek special pricing agreements from domestic vendors with their inherent paperwork or tracking costs when there is a substantial price differential versus an off-brand. If a domestic manufacturer can use the special pricing arrangement to fight an off-brand, that is a valid solution, but we believe it is tactical in nature. The price differential in off-brands versus domestic brands is too often driven by domestic costs, infrastructure, and shareholder demands, areas in which off-brands hold a distinct cost advantage.

Off-brands use the common mechanism of everyday low pricing which, with its acronym EDLP, was pioneered by Wal-Mart. The advantages of everyday low pricing strategies are obvious. Buyers do not have to file costly paperwork or use EDI sets. They can avoid legal implications and temptations from the incentive to cheat. They can rely on competitive pricing without taking title to extra inventory or keeping up with specialized sales situations that can vary widely with domestic vendors. While special pricing agreements can be effective, they are often no match for the cost advantage of off-brands. Manufacturers that try to preserve profits and market share by using special pricing agreements against qualified lower cost competition should realize their efforts are tactical and not strategic.

The profit-dollar shift, changes in purchasing processes and systems, schism in channel relationships, decreases in sales promotion, and problems with special pricing agreements will persist until off-brands capture the lion's share of the available market. In industries where off-brands are the dominant players, the channel has adjusted and the changes have taken place. In markets where off-brands are not the dominant players but are growing, these changes require study and planning.

-----

[1] Benfield, S., Vurva R.. *Restructuring the Distribution Sales Effort*, 2006, Brown Books Publishing.

[2] Greenspan, A. *The Age of Turbulence: Adventures in a New World*, 2007 Penguin: New York.

[3] Redmond, R., Ray, A., Gordon, D., "Taming the Five-Ton Elephant," *Electrical Wholesaling*, July 2007, pp. 38-41, used with permission.

[4] Johnson, Brian, Esq., "Globalization Ups Ante for Product Liability," MHEDA *Journal Online*, Summer 2005.

[5] Cicero, On Duties, pg. 71, Cambridge Press, 1991.

[6] Law Encyclopedia information about Robinson-Patman Act, *West's Encyclopedia of American Law*, 1998, Gale Group Publications.

Change Looks More Attractive than the Alternative: Where Do I Go from Here?

Reacting to these challenges requires not reacting. It requires a thoughtful and insightful review of a firm's strategy, accounting practices, financial management, organizational structure, value stream, and capacity to formulate and implement change efforts.

Segment, Segment, Segment

Offshore, off-brand competitors have focused, at least to date, on the most commoditized, price sensitive, and standardized products, which require little of the value stream beyond the basics of identifying and courting customers electronically, manufacturing in low-cost areas, and delivering worldwide. The niceties of customer support, engineering assistance, promotional assistance, and other ostensibly value-added services are not required, demanded, or valued. It is imperative that the manufacturers of products under attack by these competitors segment their businesses. Indeed, they must treat the standardized, commoditized portions of their operations as entirely separate businesses, free from the culture, traditions, mindsets, and paradigms that have grown up in the traditional environment and that now threaten to sink the firm as the competitive environment changes. We will focus first on developing strategies for this new, globalized business. However, assuming that recasting the strategy for this segment of the business is sufficient would be a tragic error. It is, as mathematicians and logicians say, necessary but not sufficient. Business history is replete with examples of low-cost, offshore competitors that enter the market with basic, feature-free products and services and then move upward to higher priced, higher value, and more fully featured products. We need look no further than Toyota, whose Lexus brand and Lexus dealerships have come a great distance from the basic Toyota Corolla beachhead with which they established their presence in North America. This phenomenon is not limited to consumer goods. Perhaps one of the most familiar to readers who travel for business is that of Embraer, the Brazilian aircraft manufacturer. Starting with the simple, cheap, unpressurized, 19-seat Bandeirante commuter aircraft, Embraer has grown its presence in the regional aircraft industry to the point that it now offers a complete line of regional jets with capacities ranging from 35 seats to 122 seats. Embraer is now challenging not only Bombardier, whose Canadair Regional Jets created the market, but Airbus and Boeing as well. As the products increased in sophistication and capability, so have Embraer's support services, which now meet the expectations of airlines worldwide.

Once a strategy has been developed for the low-end segment, the same principles must be applied to the more service-intensive and technologically sophisticated segments. Failing to do so will simply invite offshore competition in these segments, as they provide support services through websites, online, live-chat help mechanisms, call centers, and video conferencing.

A Strategy for the New Reality

A systematic approach to the review and formulation of a strategy to compete in the world of the offshore, off-brand threat is essential. We favor the widely used and highly regarded tools developed and popularized by Robert Kaplan and David Norton, originators of the Balanced Scorecard methodology.[1] Kaplan and Norton's Strategy Maps[2] give us a useful framework with which to carry out this process. A detailed examination of the formulation of strategy is beyond the scope of this book. Our purpose here is to review the elements of strategy formulation as they apply specifically to the issue of offshore and off-brand competition. We urge the reader to refer to the various works by Kaplan and Norton for a more complete treatise on the subject. In any event, it is more important that the reader employ a well thought-out process that begins with a thorough knowledge of the wants and needs of the market than to adhere to a specific model.

We begin by specifying the financial goals for the distribution channel business. We next move to a complete understanding of the perspective of the customer, specifying the value proposition that will be offered to distributors and, in turn, to their customers. We then move on to an examination of the internal processes, or value streams, that will be required to produce the specified value proposition while attaining the financial targets. Finally, we review the capabilities required to implement the necessary processes and to assess the availability of these capabilities within the firm and formulate plans to acquire the necessary capabilities or outsource the functions to specialists.

Rethinking the Finances of the Distribution-Oriented Business

We begin first with the recognition that offshore competitors are not encumbered with corporate overheads, allocated costs, executive salaries, country club membership fees, and the costs of corporate jets. Neither should your distribution channel business be weighted down with these expenses. Start with a clean piece of paper and believable data that details the true market price of these commodities and the size of the market for them. Two of Sheth's[3] self-destructive habits are likely to appear here–denial and myopia. The Sales function is likely to overestimate the market place pricing, discounting the data as an aberration, a set of special circumstances, and to discount the threat from these nontraditional competitors. The Marketing function is likely to underestimate the size of the market at risk to these competitors and to discount the data that shows that bundling "value added" offerings and similar attempts at price maintenance will not work. A ruthless disregard for traditional thinking will be required if the strategy is to be successful. Consider this to be a standalone business, and develop revenue forecasts based on the most conservative pricing and volume assumptions you can muster. Next, develop a net income estimate based on a very conservative percentage of sales. Remember that Asian companies typically take the long view and are more satisfied with smaller net income percentages than are Western companies. Because most of the offshore competition is Asian, you will be competing against societies with a dramatically longer-term orientation than the typical American quarter-to-quarter planning horizon. If your corporate culture, investors, or the analysts that follow your company can't stomach this reality, then prepare to yield the part of your business that goes through distribution to the overseas competition.

Many Western, and particularly American, companies stumble here, unable to accept the reality that a successful strategy will likely result in the repricing downward of a significant part of their businesses. This is often a portion that has traditionally been high-margin and has subsidized other lower margin businesses. The choice is clear but not particularly pleasant. Manufacturers can recognize the dramatically declining prices and margins in these businesses, accept the impact on total revenue and strategize accordingly, or succumb to paralysis and cede the business to the competition with worse results and the prospect that it will become a beachhead from which these competitors will attack the remaining profitable segments.

With the knowledge that everything related to the conduct of this business must be paid for out of the difference between your projected top and bottom lines, we can proceed with the development of the strategy. In doing so, our objective will be to formulate a strategy and, in fact, a business plan for a business whose cost structure and asset base have been dramatically reduced and designed to fit the new realities of revenue and income. We will return to the financial projections, but as we proceed, it is useful to maintain the mindset of a startup business short on cash and looking for the best deals on everything. The cost of every support function—information technology, payroll, accounting, shipping, warehousing space and others— must be capped at the lowest cost available in the marketplace. If you can get it cheaper on the outside than from your in-house functions, then do so. In any case, pay the in-house functions no more than the best outsourced price you can find. Chief financial officers, controllers, and accountants will cringe at the thought of the overhead of these functions spread over fewer dollars, people, transactions, or whatever the basis of the allocation is. The extra cost to be borne by the other business segments is the penalty paid by the firm for maintaining high-cost and less than fully utilized services. The good news in all this is that, though revenues and gross profit margins may decline, if done correctly, the leaner asset base of a recast business can result in attractive returns on assets and investment.

Many years ago, one of the authors worked with Caterpillar dealers as they struggled to come to terms with the lower revenue and lower margin lift-truck business after Caterpillar bought the Towmotor Corporation. Dealers wisely resisted adding to their asset base by building separate facilities. However, they often erred in charging to the lift-truck business the overhead of the existing earthmoving business. The lift-truck business could not stand, for example, the overhead of huge earthmoving service shops complete with overhead cranes and ten inches of concrete designed to service much larger equipment. The dual-line dealers chronically complained about the low profitability of the lift-truck business when the issue was, in reality, the misallocation of overhead and assets to a business that could neither use nor absorb them. These excess costs should have been charged to the earthmoving business as its penalty for failing to fully utilize them.

Caterpillar, it seems, faced many of the same issues, eventually selling 90% of the lift-truck business to Mitsubishi to form Mitsubishi Caterpillar Forklift America.

The Value Proposition – Giving Distributors What They Want and Will Pay For

Clayton M. Christensen pioneered and popularized the concept of disruptive technological change.[4] He argued that many technologically based firms cannot resist the temptation to continually add features and, therefore, cost to their products in a misguided attempt to gain differentiation. In many cases, he maintained, this temptation results in products that over-shoot the mark and became too sophisticated, too costly, and too capable for the majority of the market, which wants products that are cheaper and "good enough." Disruptive technology targets this large, "good enough" segment where a modicum of capability at a good price is what customers want. We argue that this same phenomenon has occurred in distribution channels where services, features, promotional efforts, sales forces, and similar accoutrements have been added that no longer confer value to distributors or users, particularly in the price-sensitive commodity segments.

Arguably, the most important portion of the strategy formulation process is the identification of those elements the customer, which is the distributor, and in turn, his customer, wants and values (read: is willing to pay for) and those that have traditionally been offered but no longer confer value. This confluence of desired product attributes, services, prices, and similar attributes define the *value proposition*. The objective is to disrupt the channel in the same fashion that disruptive products alter competition by offering only those elements that the customer values. The survey results noted earlier provide valuable guidance here.

Segment, Segment, Segment, and Segment Some More

Nowhere is this classic marketing advice more important than in designing a business that can deal with the threat of offshore sourcing. We begin with the development of a Product-Market Matrix as shown in Figure 10-1.

Figure 10-1 Product Market Matrix

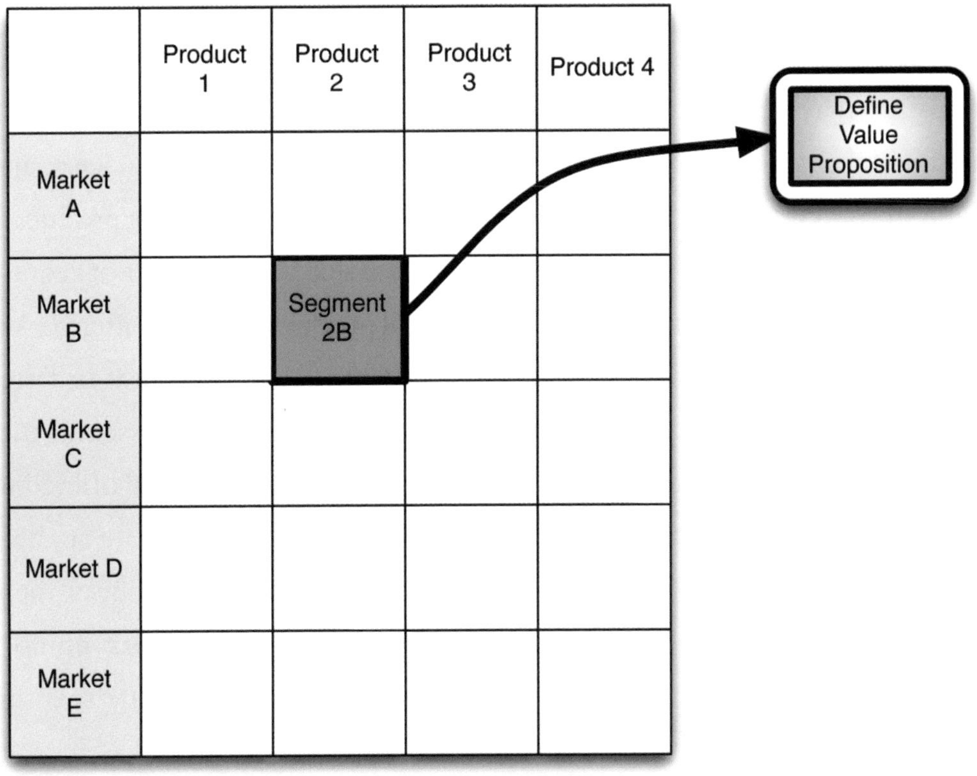

	Product 1	Product 2	Product 3	Product 4
Market A				
Market B		Segment 2B		
Market C				
Market D				
Market E				

Define Value Proposition

Our objective here is to identify unique intersections of products and markets where we can identify unique value propositions. The *market* element of this matrix is critical to the success of this process. Many industrial firms, particularly manufacturers, have a penchant for defining their businesses in terms of *products* and *product families*. While this is a useful classification, it is not sufficient to adequately define the value proposition. This concept is particularly important as we include channel activities in the concept of value proposition. For example, defining a business in terms of categories of valve products, their sophistication, technical complexity, and similar product attributes defines only a portion of the value proposition. Technically complex valves may require more technical support than more standardized commodity products. However, the nature of this assistance, as well as other non-product attributes like delivery, warranty expectations and the like, may be more related to the market into which a product is sold. Continuing with the valve example, sophisticated valves sold into process and petrochemical industries may be similar and, indeed, functionally equivalent. However, the nature of the technical assistance, the qualifications of the sales engineers, and the industry certifications may vary by the market into which the product is sold. Similarly, identical valves sold as parts of major projects will not require short lead-times or rapid delivery. The identical product sold as an aftermarket replacement may require extremely short lead-times and overnight or faster delivery to avoid disabling a major production facility. Thus, it is essential that we develop an understanding of the value proposition that will be offered to each segment. Segmentation methods can include how products are applied, how they are serviced, or their total acquisition cost. In some instances, there will be segments of economic buyers or customers who want the least number of services and product variation. Hence, an open mind and time spent in developing and testing individual segment methods is essential.

It's Only Valuable if Somebody Will Pay for It

This portion of the process must include as much customer input as possible. The temptation will be to depend on traditional wisdom, corporate legends, and myths propagated by the Sales, Marketing, and Engineering functions. Those charged with developing this strategy must solicit direct, unfiltered customer input in order to define the value proposition. For large enough segments, particularly those where key customers are located, we suggest the use of a formal process for determining and prioritizing the desires of the customer. Of course, customers would always opt for better performance, faster delivery, and lower prices if they could have them all. Identifying and forcing the trade-offs with an explicit process such as Quality Function Deployment can force customers to prioritize their desires and aid in the development of the value proposition. Most importantly, it will aid in the identification of those nice-to-have attributes and services that customers won't pay for and you shouldn't provide simply because you always have.

Let's turn to another example that can be used to illustrate this relationship between what is important and what customers are willing to pay for. The same manufacturer of industrial products mentioned above maintained a long-standing policy of same-day shipment of many of their products. Because of the wide variation in the product, this frequently required extraordinary manufacturing efforts to produce small lots of unique products on a special second-shift operation. It also required Herculean efforts to ensure shipment, which included special arrangements with UPS for late pickups at the manufacturing facility. As UPS and FedEx both learned early on, customers will always opt for better service if there is no extra charge for it. Now, if you want it by 10:30 p.m., you pay more than you do if 2 p.m. or 4 p.m. is adequate. The manufacturer in our example levied no additional charge for the same-day manufacture and shipment of products, but maintained it was a key element in the value offered to the customer (in this case, distributors) and a key competitive element. An analysis of the orders for these products revealed that only 21% of them were specified to be shipped via overnight express. Eighty percent of these high-cost, lower margin orders were shipped by UPS ground or LTL freight and sat in trucks for several days before their eventual arrival! What the manufacturer thought was a value-add was only a cost-add. We recommended that an expediting charge be added, and all of these shipments be made via FedEx Priority Overnight or UPS Air in an effort to identify those customers who valued the service enough to pay for it.

Few of them did. In spite of years of tradition, this service was not part of the value proposition because most customers wouldn't pay for it. Capabilities, services, and features *become part of the value proposition when they add value that customers will pay for.*

As this is being written, Apple Incorporated is enjoying the success of its iPhone, with close to one million sold in the first two months of sales. At the same time, surveys are revealing that a growing portion of the market for cell phones wants what Christensen called "disruptive technology.[5] For this segment, a phone with only the ability to make and receive calls is "good enough." Offering this group an iPhone offers them no additional value, and they will not pay for it. Conversely, technophiles and "road warriors" have lined up to purchase iPhones, and numerous people are "hacking" it to use with other networks and outside the United States. For this group, the unique features of the iPhone add value for which they are willing to pay the $499 to $599 price. Cutting the price to attract the former group may work, but it is better to design a product/service system that meets their needs and for which they will pay a profitable price.

Value Means Uniqueness

In addition to determining the product attributes and services that the customer will pay for, firms must identify those that only they can provide or that they can provide better than anyone else. We are looking for a competitive advantage, a unique value proposition that sets the firm apart from its competition. Whatever unique value proposition you settle on, it must also be sustainable. A product feature or customer service element that can be duplicated easily, quickly, and at low cost is not a sustainable advantage. Something that is expensive, hard to duplicate, and which requires a lengthy process to implement may, in fact, be a sustaining advantage, but only if the market segment values it.

What the Firm Does—the Value Stream

Having identified the attributes—both product and service—that add value to distributors and users, the firm must develop the capability to develop and deliver them. We focus on those capabilities that the firm can do or learn to do better than anyone else. The value stream concept, popularized by Michael Porter[6] and now widely used as an insightful way to view the functions of an organization, is a useful tool here. Simply stated, the core value stream is the stream of individual processes that must be accomplished for the firm to identify and acquire customers, secure orders, receive inbound inputs (materials, labor, information, etc.), process these inputs, deliver the product or service, and receive payment. Supporting services include those functions that permit the core functions to operate (accounting, human resources, legal, and other traditionally staff-support functions).

A Value Stream for Each Segment

Having identified the essential elements of the value proposition for each segment, we are faced with a multifaceted task. First, we have to identify the value stream that currently provides products and services to the segment.

Figure 10-2 Segment Value Stream

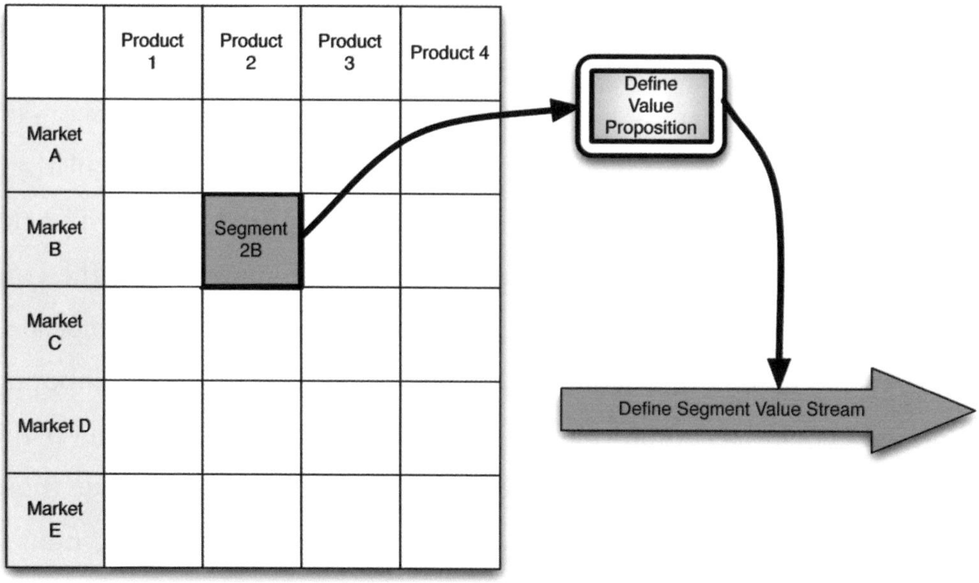

The temptation will undoubtedly be to immediately go beyond this step. We caution against this approach. Examining the present value stream permits the identification of those activities currently being performed and adding cost to the products and services. More importantly, it allows a comparison of what is currently being done with what we have determined— or preferably what the customers who occupy this segment have told us— adds value that will command a price.

Ruthlessness is the key principle as this comparison between what is and what needs to be is carried out. Habits, corporate myths, sacred cows, and change resistance will conspire to classify everything as essential and key to competitiveness. In our experience, this process will be reminiscent of budget-cutting exercises. Everything will be seen as absolutely essential and unable to be eliminated. Face-to-face sales calls on distributors handling commodity product will suddenly take on strategic importance. Elaborate sales promotion material, technical training classes, instant sales engineering assistance, and similar "cost adders" will become the key to survival in even those segments where the most basic of products are being offered. How essential to competitiveness in selling cast iron pipe fittings is technical information, on site sales representation, and sales promotion? Their functions and specifications are well known, the applications are static, and no amount of sales promotion can induce people who don't need fittings to buy them. If your offshore competitor doesn't do it, it is a good clue that it is unnecessary. WalMart's "Every Day Low Prices" is the watchword for these commoditized product/market segments.

Value Migration—Skating to Where the Puck Will Be

Conversely, more technically demanding and sophisticated markets offer opportunities to incorporate value-added advantages into the value stream. New products, new applications of existing products, highly sophisticated products, and those products sold into segments where their correct application is essential but difficult offer opportunities to add value and delay the offshore competitors' moves up-market. In these cases, the value will have migrated from the simple product to the systems required to specify, acquire, and apply it effectively—that is, to the knowledge-adding portion of the value chain. Many years ago, when IBM first introduced the outrageously priced personal computer of the day, margins in the design and manufacture of the hardware were substantial. Value has now migrated in the value chain to the point where the product of knowledge work–software— earns the largest margins, followed by distribution. (Lest you be told otherwise, Dell is a distributor, not a manufacturer, and Apple's per-square-foot profits in their retail stores are the envy of the retail world.) Similarly, in these more sophisticated segments, manufacturers and their distributors can add value by focusing on those portions of the value chain that cannot be done remotely with ease and panache. Training, application assistance, and similar functions that are done best with knowledgeable, experienced people are naturals as competitive weapons with which to differentiate a firm from offshore businesses. There is a nascent trend to move call centers and similar customer service functions back on shore as the result of increased dissatisfaction with the level of support that can be offered by offshore installations. There is a growing body of opinion that holds that complicated transactions, troubleshooting, and other interactions that cannot easily be reduced to menu-driven procedures may more effectively be done in the United States. Avon Products Incorporated employs offshore call centers for many of the interactions with its independent representatives. However, calls from the largest and most productive representatives are routed to a domestic call center where the complexity and non-standard nature of the calls is more easily handled. We hasten to add that this is in no way a reflection upon the capability and intelligence of the offshore call center employees. It does reflect long-standing cultural prohibitions against challenging the status quo, questioning management, and improvising in many of these cultures where autocratic leadership styles have long been the norm. Given the spread of globalization, these cultural norms are likely to fade, but for the present, they offer an opportunity for domestic manufacturers to distinguish themselves with superior service in sophisticated market segments.

Summarized simply, put resources, assets, and effort in those portions of the value chain where value can be added and will be paid for *in each specific product/market segment.*

At the conclusion of this analysis, our objective is to identify, as shown in Figure 10-2, the optimum value stream for each significant product/market segment.

Merging Similar Value Chains

Firms typically find the thought of managing a multitude of individual value chains—each one catering to an individual product market/segment—to be daunting and are tempted to throw up their hands in despair at this point. Fortunately, our experience has taught us that multiple, similar value streams may be merged into a manageable number of streams, as shown in Figure 10-3. Each of these streams can be close enough to optimum for several important product/market segments that the task becomes manageable.

Figure 10-3 Merged Value Streams

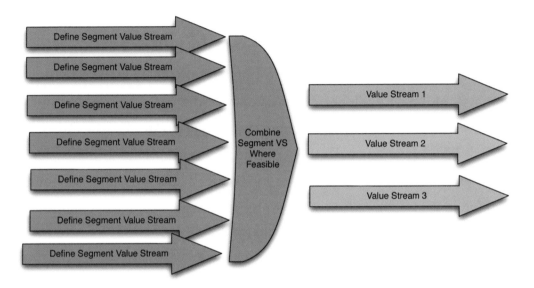

How Will You Provide What You Decide to Provide?

After deciding, undoubtedly after much debate and discussion, what to provide in the value stream for a given group of product/market segments, the next issue becomes how to provide it. To proceed, we must disaggregate the value chain for the product/market segments under consideration. Christensen[7] and others noticed that early in the life cycle of a product or business, the value stream had to be tightly integrated at the interfaces of the processes if they were to work together to deliver the desired product and service. We may return to our IBM PC example to illustrate. Early in the life of the PC, IBM had to take ownership of the various parts of the value stream to ensure that they would all work together. PC-DOS, licensed from an embryonic Microsoft, as well as a variety of early application packages were available from IBM along with the hardware. Without this integration and control of the interfaces between segments of the value stream, the product/service system would not work. As the PC matured, the interfaces no longer required this level of tight coordination, and the value chain became disaggregated, with separate players providing hardware, operating systems, application software, and distributing the various elements largely independently.

We would argue that the products handled by industrial distribution, at least those facing near-term offshore competition, fall into the category of mature products with value streams that may be disaggregated. Simply put, it is not necessary for the product manufacturer to perform all of the functions. They may be openly or covertly performed by third parties at higher levels of performance and efficiency and at lower cost. Having decided what must be done in a value stream to serve a particular segment, management must decide how it must be done and by whom.

Defining the Elements of the Business

Management and organizational theorists have argued for years about whether a business should be organized around products or markets. In this debate, markets have generally been defined as common groups of customers and, in practice, generally take the form of broad amalgamations of customers with vaguely similar businesses. Typical examples are air conditioning customers, refrigeration customers, petrochemical customers, and similar, rather generic classifications. We argue that this simplistic classification of what has come to be called "Strategic Business Units" is inadequate. Rather, we maintain, a Strategic Business Unit should be defined as one of the common value streams that results from the amalgamation of individual product/market segment value streams. Each of these combined value streams represents the processes required to provide similar value propositions to groups of customers with similar needs. This focuses each portion of the business upon satisfying a specific set of needs.

In fact, we would take this a step further and suggest that it is segment-based SBUs around which leadership, management, and profit and loss accountability should be focused. In our model, each of these amalgamated value streams should constitute at least a semi-autonomous business, and the more autonomous the better! The leader of each business, call him/her what you like and whatever fits your traditions and industry, the Product Manager, Business Leader, or Division Manager must become responsible not only for the profit and loss of the business, but for acquiring the functions necessary to make the processes work and to deliver the value represented by the value stream of his business.

Providing What Is Valued, Paying What It Is Worth

Return, if you will, to our earlier discussions of cost structures, allocation of overhead, and the recognition that many of the activities done and services provided no longer add value. The leader of each of these value-stream-oriented businesses must be completely free to provide only those products and services that add value, to carry on only those activities that contribute to the creation of this value, and to source the required processes from the entity that can provide them most cost efficiently. Let us illustrate. The business leader of Business (Value Stream) A determines that his particular business no longer required a field sales force, but instead requires a stronger online presence, improved provisions for e-commerce, sales collateral material that may be easily downloaded, and the ability to collaborate virtually with distributor or user sales engineers to assist in the specifying and application of the products. The Business Leader must be free to source each of these functions from wherever they can best be obtained, internally or externally. The sacred cows of internal marketing and information technology may have to be slain. Let us consider another example. Business Leader B determines that offshore competition will require continued cost and price reductions for a group of commodity products if the business is to retain its customers. She must be permitted to produce, purchase, or develop these products wherever necessary and possible to achieve these objectives. We are reminded of Caterpillar's decision in the early 1980s to mothball the world-class gray iron foundries that had been built in Mapleton, Illinois, just downstream from Cat's headquarters in Peoria, Illinois. Casting and foundry experts were redeployed and found their roles changing from manufacturing to sourcing, supplier qualification, and supplier development. They succeeded in finding numerous sources of high quality castings at substantial cost savings in numerous locations worldwide. The culture shock at Caterpillar was significant but prophetic. The realization at this once insular company that a world of capability existed outside the organization's walls and that this capability was often more cost-effective than the traditional internal resources was beginning to dawn. Manufacturers faced with offshore competition for their distribution channel, and perhaps other businesses, will find it imperative to employ a similar thought process.

Let us continue with our examples by presuming that Business C believes that there is an opportunity for a new type of an as-yet-undeveloped product. In our traditional organizations, this would typically mean the beginning of a traditional product development process using internal research and development, engineering, manufacturing, and other resources. If we are fortunate, our organization has learned to do this in cross-functional teams. This, however, is no longer sufficient. As Don Tapscott points out in *Wikinomics*,[8] once intensely insular Proctor & Gamble now prides itself on the proportion of new product ideas and research developments that come from outside the company, and Tapscott credits Boeing's success with the 787 Dreamliner to the company's ability to collaborate with outside developers. The leader of Business C must be free to source ideas and technology from wherever they can most quickly and effectively be obtained.

Getting It Done No Longer Means Doing It

What happens, it is reasonable to ask, to the traditional functions in this value stream-oriented organization? They become subject matter and functional experts, providing or acquiring specific skills or services. Accounting may provide accounting functions or find suitable outsourcing arrangements. Engineering may provide engineers or arrange for contract engineering and design services. Manufacturing and purchasing will merge and arrange to make, have made in a dedicated contract manufacturing operation, or outright purchase the necessary products. The traditional functions will become coordinators and collaborators, ensuring that each business unit gets what it needs from the most appropriate source in the new crowd-sourced world of global business. We end up with an organization much like that depicted in Figure 10-4.

Figure 10-4 The New Organization

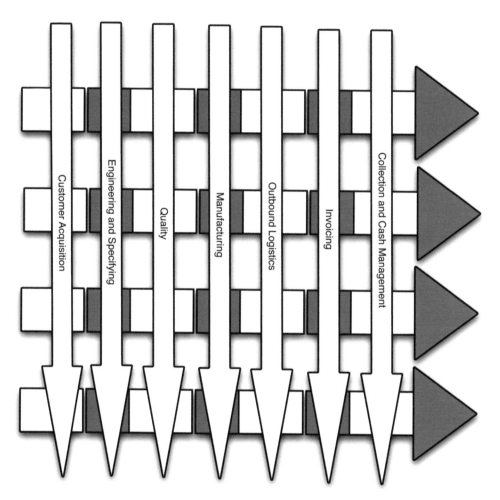

The horizontal business units intersect with the functional units that provide or arrange to acquire the services and functions that the business units are willing to purchase at prices they are willing to pay. And one final word is in order here. These intersection points represent points of collaboration between those individuals assigned to specific functions in each SBU/value stream and the subject matter experts or contract service providers represented by the vertical arrows. Indeed, you will probably find that each of these intersections forms the nucleus of one or more cross-functional teams.

Resist the temptation to make these internal functions "profit centers." Profits are only earned when goods and services are sold at arm's length to third parties. Profits are not earned when an internal function provides service to another internal entity. Making these functions profit centers simply encourages the stacking of margins with the inevitable result that the final price to the paying customer is noncompetitive. These functions are cost centers. Their services should be passed to the Business Units at cost. However, you may find that each of these groups becomes adept at providing goods and services in a quite competitive manner. Indeed, they will learn that their survival depends on it. In this case, you may find you have created a new business and are able to sell these services to third parties at a genuine profit.

If You Don't Use It, Don't Pay for It

As individuals, few of us are willing to continue to pay for functions and services that we do not value. And so it should be with the business units. Burdening these businesses with overhead allocations, the cost of uncompetitive internal "services," functions they can't use or don't want to pay for, corporate jets and memberships and similar excesses will render them permanently noncompetitive. Once the business units are operating competitively and purchasing and using only value-added goods and services at prices they can afford, add up the real profits earned by the business units, subtract the corporate overhead costs, and what is left belongs to the owner(s). If it represents an inadequate return, you have a few choices. First, you can lose some of the overhead. If the business units are paying for the services they want and can afford, then there is a real question what a lot of the corporate overhead provides. If you can't live without the Gulfstreams or Lears, then the shareholders will have to accept lower returns. The authors support the use of corporate aviation in the right circumstances. It is a wonderful time-saver in this era of chronic delays, missed connections, and general frustration. However, when a business leader sees the full cost of private jets, options like fractional ownership and web conferencing look very appealing. And when the corporate offices can't pass the costs of the jets, the clubs, the lodges, and the like to the business units, their true cost and impact on the shareholder return comes into sharp focus.

If we sound strident here, please forgive us. We would hasten to point out, however, that the Taicang City Jinxin Copper Tube Co., Ltd., or FluidFit Engineers of Mumbai are unlikely to belong to country clubs or have lodges, and the extent of their corporate aviation function is likely to be economy class tickets, often from consolidators. Their willingness or need to fund expensive customer "meetings" at far away world-class resorts is low. Welcome to the disrupted channel and the new realities of the globalized world of durable goods markets.

Dynamiting the Silos

If we redefine our business in terms of the value streams responsible for delivering a unique value proposition to groups of similar customers, what will become of the traditional functional units, those classic repositories of corporate power and influence? They become repositories of functional competence and subject matter experts whose purpose is to provide or assist in the acquisition of goods and services necessary to the value stream. Let us quickly hasten to add that we are not fans of the matrix organization where inordinate amounts of time are spent coordinating events and business leaders devote much of their energy to an inwardly focused round of negotiations whenever a decision is to be made. Our model for the distribution-oriented manufacturer of the future is definitely not a matrix. Rather, we are suggesting that these firms convert from vertical silos of functionality to horizontal pipes whose function is to allow value to flow to the customer. Decision-making occurs in the pipes, and the functional areas of expertise are charged with assisting and providing expertise and services as required. Again, it is not practical in this text to give instructions on control systems, planning, and alignment of responsibility and authority to drive segment growth. There are many theories, texts, and advisors on organizational change and management. Our purpose here is to catalog the need for change and give an overview of the key areas for change that allow the domestic manufacturer to successfully compete in the global environment.

----

[1] Kaplan, R., & Norton, D. (1996). *The Balanced Scorecard*. Boston: Harvard Business School Press.

[2] Kaplan, R., & Norton, D. (2004). *Strategy Maps*. Boston: Harvard Business School Press.

[3] Sheth, J. (2007). *The Self-Destructive Habits of Good Companies...and How to Break Them*. Upper Saddle River, NJ: Pearson Education Inc.

[4] Christensen, C. (1997). *The Innovator's Dilemma*. Boston: Harvard Business School Press.

[5] Ibid.

[6] Porter, M. (1985). *Competitive Advantage: Creating and Sustaining Superior Performance*. New York: The Free Press.

[7] Christensen, C. (1997). *The Innovator's Dilemma*. Boston: Harvard Business School Press.

[8] Tapscott, D., & Williams, A. (2006). *Wikinomics: How Mass Collaboration Changes Everything*. New York: Penguin Press.

CHAPTER eleven

A Word About Change

We are well aware that the changes we have documented, including the strategic challenges facing both distributors and manufacturers, constitute substantive change. The actions we have suggested for meeting these challenges represent fundamental and significant modification to the way business is conducted. Dealing with foreign suppliers, dramatically revising the way costs are accounted for, and changing the very way these businesses are organized represent nothing less than gut-wrenching but very necessary changes. We are also aware that research shows that some 70% of all organizational change efforts fail to achieve the lasting structure necessary to allow the organizations to adapt, survive, and prosper. This failure is so pervasive that we suggest you consult John Kotter's seminal article *Leading Change: Why Transformational Efforts Fail.*[1] Are we suggesting, then, actions that are doomed to failure? We do not think so. We are, however, suggesting actions that will be difficult to achieve and that will require hard work and concentrated effort of a kind that is different from much of that expended in these organizations. They will require leadership rather than management. While you may not wish to confront the global environment, the speed of transformation caused by off-brands will likely bring financial hardship to those who don't address the issues.

Leading the Change—Plan the Change Effort Before the Change

We suggest that, if you are reading this, you have recognized that there is something fundamentally different about the environment your business will be facing in the future. You have recognized that your organization must change to meet these challenges and, we hope, have developed a sense of urgency surrounding these alterations. Your first and most important task will be to foster the same sense of urgency among your colleagues. This study is our effort to help you do this. The biggest challenge you will face is the need to convince others around you of the urgency of change. This inertia, or *stasis momentum* as organizational development experts call it, is arguably the single most powerful obstacle to organizational change. Human beings, as a rule, resist change until the current situation becomes unbearably uncomfortable or so fraught with peril that it is easier to change than to remain in the current state. Your job will be to create this sense of discomfort and fear, if you believe as we do that these fundamental changes to durable goods channels present a clear and present danger to organizations that fail to change.

Share this material with those in your organization whom you believe share your views, no matter how nascent their beliefs are. Gather around you a coalition of those who, regardless of their position in the organization, believe that these changes are real and adaptation is necessary for the survival of your industrial distribution business. This coalition should include opinion makers and individuals whose competence and judgment are respected. Ideally, it will include individuals of some stature in the firm. If not, your coalition's first task will be to convince those in positions of power that these changes are real and threatening. If those in power are sated and feel no need to lead change, your first task may be to change *them*.

This change coalition must develop—as a team and with much consultation, debate, communication, and discussion—a clear understanding of two situations. First, you must understand and be able to clearly communicate the current state of your business—where it is strong and where it is weak, and where you believe it is inadequate to deal with the challenges of globalization. Next, using the tools and concepts introduced above and, ideally, with some outside help that can bring fresh perspectives to your effort, develop your team's vision for the future state of your organization.

Resist the immediate temptation to begin putting plans, schedules, and projects into place to bring about these changes. There is far more groundwork to do at this stage. You must communicate your vision as widely and as often as you can to as large an audience as you can manage within your organization. This audience must become convinced of the need to change, the inadequacy of the current state of the organization, and the desirability of the envisioned future state. Do not consider your future state to be definitive at this point. Rather, consider it to be a straw-man proposal put forth for discussion and refinement. Change efforts promulgated from above or from a small group viewed as the chosen few in the know are famous for their likelihood of failure. You and your like-minded group of change agents will be impatient to begin the implementation. Resist this impatience. Study after study has shown that the wider the participation in the development of the future vision and the more frequent the communication on the subject of the changes and the desired future state, the more successful the eventual change will be. Time spent in the early stages of change efforts toward improving participation and communication—the two most important antecedents to change—pays real dividends in the eventual speed and sustainability of the organizational change.

As a change leader in your organization, we urge you to spend the time necessary to acquaint yourself with the discipline of organizational change. Learn about change from the vast wealth of resources available on the subject. Kotter's works, both in article and book form, will be priceless to your effort. Only after managing this leadership effort should you turn to the work of management, which involves developing the detailed plans, schedules, programs, and budgets necessary to bring about your future state. We wish you the best of luck and the greatest success in your endeavors.

---

[1] Kotter, J. (1995) "Leading Change: Why Transformation Efforts Fail." Harvard Business Review, March-April 1995.

CHAPTER

twelve

A Word About Statistics and the Reliability of the Survey

One reasonable question that the reader may and arguably should ask is just how much stock to put into the results of the survey. Can a survey with some 200 respondents really reveal the thinking of the entire population of durable goods distributors? Fortunately, there are proven, quantitative methods with which to measure just how much predictive validity this survey possesses.

A perfectly trustworthy survey requires two essential elements. First, the sample of respondents must be randomly selected from the entire population of interest. In this case, the distributor personnel asked to respond would have been randomly drawn from a list of all distributor managers and executives. In practice, such complete randomness is difficult if not impossible to achieve. This survey was made available to the entire readership of *Progressive Distributor* magazine. Those who responded did so voluntarily and without any further selection mechanism than basic interest in the subject. While not strictly random, such convenience sampling, as it is called, is considered to be adequate, particularly when the sample size is large enough. Furthermore, the respondents were spread across dozens of distinct durable goods vertical markets.

The second major criteria for reliability is a sample of adequate size. Statistical theory and practice tell us that when dealing with mean or average scores as we are here, a sample size of 30 or greater is sufficient. The actual sample size, which approached 200 (varying slightly from question to question) is many times greater than the minimum, and therefore, contributes to enhanced confidence in our results.

In order to test our methods and conclusions, we conducted statistical tests to calculate the confidence interval of the bulk of the questions. For example, in Question 5 of the survey, we asked respondents to tell us the trend in offshore purchases they were experiencing along a four point scale that ranged from 1 – "Declined" to 4 – "Increased Significantly." The mean score was 3.38, or approximately one third of the way between "Increased Slightly" and "Increased Significantly." The relevant question is how well this mean sample score predicts the actual mean score that would be recorded if all the distributors on the *Progressive Distributor* mailing list responded to this question. Fortunately, readily available statistical tests and software can answer this question. We construct what is known as a "confidence interval" around the mean score of 3.38 at a confidence level of 95%. In this case, the 95% confidence interval extends from 3.27 to 3.49. Statisticians interpret this to mean that 95% of the samples drawn from the population of all distributors would have a mean within this very tight range. Figure 12-1 illustrates the output from the JMP statistical software package.

From a practical standpoint, this result tells us that we can be 95% confident that the mean score on this question, if answered by all distributors, would be within our confidence interval of 3.27 - 3.49. Therefore, we can conclude that the survey is a highly accurate predictor of the responses of distributors in general. Similar tests were conducted for other questions for which multiple responses were not permitted. The results with statistical software output for selected questions of particular interest are shown in detail in the Appendix. Based on these results, we are confident that the results of the survey are an accurate portrayal of overall durable goods distributor attitudes and experiences.

Figure 12-1

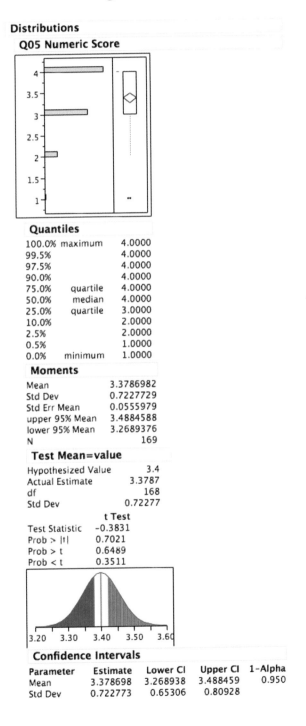

Distributions

Q05 Numeric Score

Quantiles

100.0%	maximum	4.0000
99.5%		4.0000
97.5%		4.0000
90.0%		4.0000
75.0%	quartile	4.0000
50.0%	median	4.0000
25.0%	quartile	3.0000
10.0%		2.0000
2.5%		2.0000
0.5%		1.0000
0.0%	minimum	1.0000

Moments

Mean	3.3786982
Std Dev	0.7227729
Std Err Mean	0.0555979
upper 95% Mean	3.4884588
lower 95% Mean	3.2689376
N	169

Test Mean=value

Hypothesized Value	3.4
Actual Estimate	3.3787
df	168
Std Dev	0.72277

t Test

Test Statistic	-0.3831
Prob > |t|	0.7021
Prob > t	0.6489
Prob < t	0.3511

Confidence Intervals

Parameter	Estimate	Lower CI	Upper CI	1–Alpha
Mean	3.378698	3.268938	3.488459	0.950
Std Dev	0.722773	0.65306	0.80928	

APPENDIX

Review of Selected Statistical Tests of Interest

Distributor Perception of Customer Attitude Toward Off-brand Items

Importance to Distributors of Timely Delivery by Offshore Suppliers

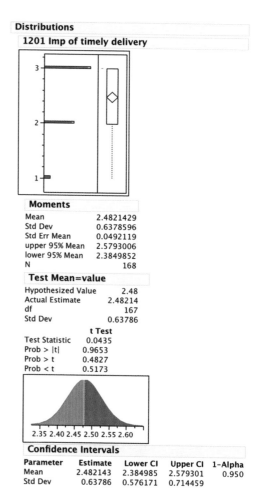

Distributions

Q10 Numeric Score

Moments

Mean	2.5833333
Std Dev	0.9051858
Std Err Mean	0.0698366
upper 95% Mean	2.7212097
lower 95% Mean	2.445457
N	168

Test Mean=value

Hypothesized Value	2.58
Actual Estimate	2.58333
df	167
Std Dev	0.90519

t Test

Test Statistic	0.0477
Prob > |t|	0.9620
Prob > t	0.4810
Prob < t	0.5190

Confidence Intervals

Parameter	Estimate	Lower CI	Upper CI	1–Alpha
Mean	2.583333	2.445457	2.72121	0.950
Std Dev	0.905186	0.817643	1.013887	

Distributions

1201 Imp of timely delivery

Moments

Mean	2.4821429
Std Dev	0.6378596
Std Err Mean	0.0492119
upper 95% Mean	2.5793006
lower 95% Mean	2.3849852
N	168

Test Mean=value

Hypothesized Value	2.48
Actual Estimate	2.48214
df	167
Std Dev	0.63786

t Test

Test Statistic	0.0435
Prob > |t|	0.9653
Prob > t	0.4827
Prob < t	0.5173

Confidence Intervals

Parameter	Estimate	Lower CI	Upper CI	1–Alpha
Mean	2.482143	2.384985	2.579301	0.950
Std Dev	0.63786	0.576171	0.714459	

Importance to Distributors of Product Literature

Importance to Distributors of Warranty and Return Privileges

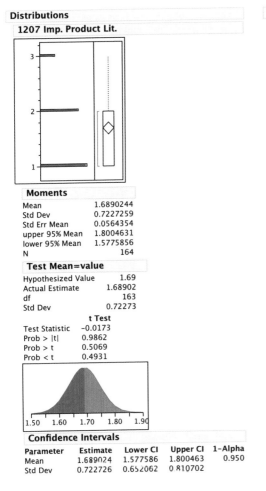

Distributions

1207 Imp. Product Lit.

Moments

Mean	1.6890244
Std Dev	0.7227259
Std Err Mean	0.0564354
upper 95% Mean	1.8004631
lower 95% Mean	1.5775856
N	164

Test Mean=value

Hypothesized Value	1.69
Actual Estimate	1.68902
df	163
Std Dev	0.72273

t Test

Test Statistic	-0.0173
Prob > |t|	0.9862
Prob > t	0.5069
Prob < t	0.4931

Confidence Intervals

Parameter	Estimate	Lower CI	Upper CI	1-Alpha
Mean	1.689024	1.577586	1.800463	0.950
Std Dev	0.722726	0.652062	0.810702	

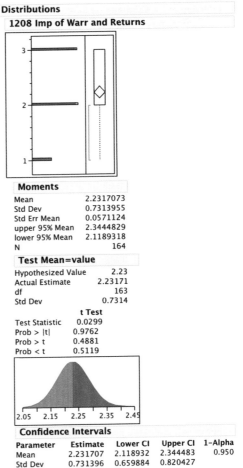

Distributions

1208 Imp of Warr and Returns

Moments

Mean	2.2317073
Std Dev	0.7313955
Std Err Mean	0.0571124
upper 95% Mean	2.3444829
lower 95% Mean	2.1189318
N	164

Test Mean=value

Hypothesized Value	2.23
Actual Estimate	2.23171
df	163
Std Dev	0.7314

t Test

Test Statistic	0.0299
Prob > |t|	0.9762
Prob > t	0.4881
Prob < t	0.5119

Confidence Intervals

Parameter	Estimate	Lower CI	Upper CI	1-Alpha
Mean	2.231707	2.118932	2.344483	0.950
Std Dev	0.731396	0.659884	0.820427	

Importance to Distributors of Product and Application Training

Importance to Distributors of Certifications and Code Approvals

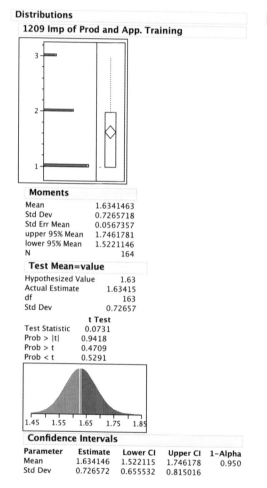

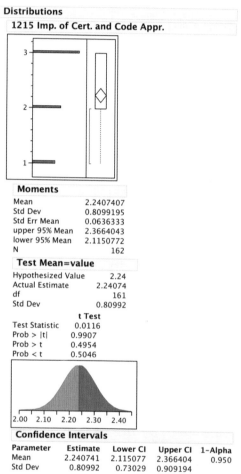

Distributions

1209 Imp of Prod and App. Training

Moments

Mean	1.6341463
Std Dev	0.7265718
Std Err Mean	0.0567357
upper 95% Mean	1.7461781
lower 95% Mean	1.5221146
N	164

Test Mean=value

Hypothesized Value	1.63
Actual Estimate	1.63415
df	163
Std Dev	0.72657

t Test

Test Statistic	0.0731
Prob > |t|	0.9418
Prob > t	0.4709
Prob < t	0.5291

Confidence Intervals

Parameter	Estimate	Lower CI	Upper CI	1-Alpha
Mean	1.634146	1.522115	1.746178	0.950
Std Dev	0.726572	0.655532	0.815016	

Distributions

1215 Imp. of Cert. and Code Appr.

Moments

Mean	2.2407407
Std Dev	0.8099195
Std Err Mean	0.0636333
upper 95% Mean	2.3664043
lower 95% Mean	2.1150772
N	162

Test Mean=value

Hypothesized Value	2.24
Actual Estimate	2.24074
df	161
Std Dev	0.80992

t Test

Test Statistic	0.0116
Prob > |t|	0.9907
Prob > t	0.4954
Prob < t	0.5046

Confidence Intervals

Parameter	Estimate	Lower CI	Upper CI	1-Alpha
Mean	2.240741	2.115077	2.366404	0.950
Std Dev	0.80992	0.73029	0.909194	

Foreign Supplier Timely Delivery vs. Domestic Suppliers

Quality of Field Sales Support vs. Domestic Suppliers

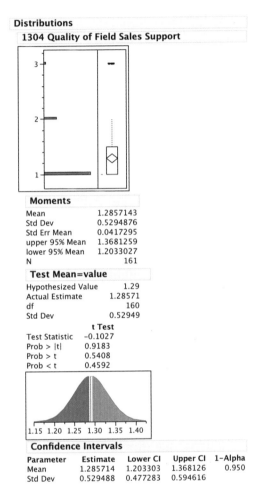

Distributions

1301 Delivery Perf.

Moments

Mean	1.6707317
Std Dev	0.7102212
Std Err Mean	0.055459
upper 95% Mean	1.7802423
lower 95% Mean	1.5612211
N	164

Test Mean=value

Hypothesized Value	1.67
Actual Estimate	1.67073
df	163
Std Dev	0.71022

t Test

Test Statistic	0.0132
Prob > |t|	0.9895
Prob > t	0.4947
Prob < t	0.5053

1.50 1.60 1.70 1.80

Confidence Intervals

Parameter	Estimate	Lower CI	Upper CI	1–Alpha
Mean	1.670732	1.561221	1.780242	0.950
Std Dev	0.710221	0.64078	0.796675	

Distributions

1304 Quality of Field Sales Support

Moments

Mean	1.2857143
Std Dev	0.5294876
Std Err Mean	0.0417295
upper 95% Mean	1.3681259
lower 95% Mean	1.2033027
N	161

Test Mean=value

Hypothesized Value	1.29
Actual Estimate	1.28571
df	160
Std Dev	0.52949

t Test

Test Statistic	-0.1027
Prob > |t|	0.9183
Prob > t	0.5408
Prob < t	0.4592

1.15 1.20 1.25 1.30 1.35 1.40

Confidence Intervals

Parameter	Estimate	Lower CI	Upper CI	1–Alpha
Mean	1.285714	1.203303	1.368126	0.950
Std Dev	0.529488	0.477283	0.594616	

Quality of Technical Support vs. Domestic Suppliers

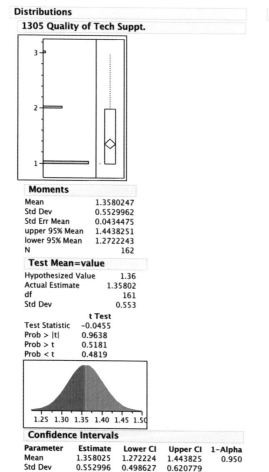

Distributions

1305 Quality of Tech Suppt.

Moments

Mean	1.3580247
Std Dev	0.5529962
Std Err Mean	0.0434475
upper 95% Mean	1.4438251
lower 95% Mean	1.2722243
N	162

Test Mean=value

Hypothesized Value	1.36
Actual Estimate	1.35802
df	161
Std Dev	0.553

t Test

Test Statistic	-0.0455
Prob > |t|	0.9638
Prob > t	0.5181
Prob < t	0.4819

Confidence Intervals

Parameter	Estimate	Lower CI	Upper CI	1-Alpha
Mean	1.358025	1.272224	1.443825	0.950
Std Dev	0.552996	0.498627	0.620779	

Quality of Certifications and Approvals vs. Domestic Suppliers

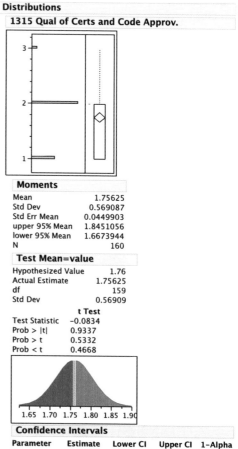

Distributions

1315 Qual of Certs and Code Approv.

Moments

Mean	1.75625
Std Dev	0.569087
Std Err Mean	0.0449903
upper 95% Mean	1.8451056
lower 95% Mean	1.6673944
N	160

Test Mean=value

Hypothesized Value	1.76
Actual Estimate	1.75625
df	159
Std Dev	0.56909

t Test

Test Statistic	-0.0834
Prob > |t|	0.9337
Prob > t	0.5332
Prob < t	0.4668

Confidence Intervals

Parameter	Estimate	Lower CI	Upper CI	1-Alpha
Mean	1.75625	1.667394	1.845106	0.950
Std Dev	0.569087	0.51282	0.639332	

Distributor Perception of Brand Importance

Distributor Interest in Private Labels

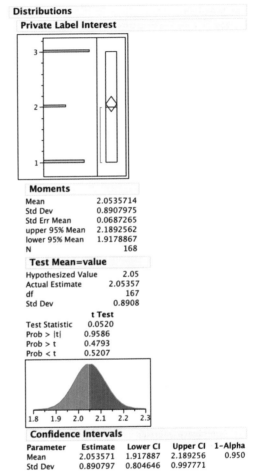

Distributions

q14 Brand Power

Moments

Mean	3.0235294
Std Dev	0.6789562
Std Err Mean	0.0520736
upper 95% Mean	3.1263279
lower 95% Mean	2.920731
N	170

Test Mean=value

Hypothesized Value	3.02
Actual Estimate	3.02353
df	169
Std Dev	0.67896

t Test

Test Statistic	0.0678
Prob > |t|	0.9460
Prob > t	0.4730
Prob < t	0.5270

Confidence Intervals

Parameter	Estimate	Lower CI	Upper CI	1-Alpha
Mean	3.023529	2.920731	3.126328	0.950
Std Dev	0.678956	0.613644	0.75995	

Distributions

Private Label Interest

Moments

Mean	2.0535714
Std Dev	0.8907975
Std Err Mean	0.0687265
upper 95% Mean	2.1892562
lower 95% Mean	1.9178867
N	168

Test Mean=value

Hypothesized Value	2.05
Actual Estimate	2.05357
df	167
Std Dev	0.8908

t Test

Test Statistic	0.0520
Prob > |t|	0.9586
Prob > t	0.4793
Prob < t	0.5207

Confidence Intervals

Parameter	Estimate	Lower CI	Upper CI	1-Alpha
Mean	2.053571	1.917887	2.189256	0.950
Std Dev	0.890797	0.804646	0.997771	

Distributor Actively Seeking Offshore Relationships

Distributor Perception of Customer Satisfaction with Offshore Products

Distributions

Q20 Actively Seeking Offshore Relationships

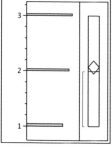

Moments

Mean	2.0718563
Std Dev	0.8108367
Std Err Mean	0.0627444
upper 95% Mean	2.1957362
lower 95% Mean	1.9479763
N	167

Test Mean=value

Hypothesized Value	2.07
Actual Estimate	2.07186
df	166
Std Dev	0.81084

t Test

Test Statistic	0.0296
Prob > |t|	0.9764
Prob > t	0.4882
Prob < t	0.5118

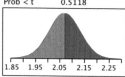

Confidence Intervals

Parameter	Estimate	Lower CI	Upper CI	1–Alpha
Mean	2.071856	1.947976	2.195736	0.950
Std Dev	0.810837	0.732206	0.908536	

Distributions

Q21 Cust Happy with Offshore Product

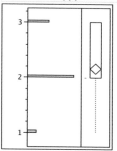

Moments

Mean	2.1607143
Std Dev	0.612547
Std Err Mean	0.047259
upper 95% Mean	2.2540164
lower 95% Mean	2.0674122
N	168

Test Mean=value

Hypothesized Value	2.16
Actual Estimate	2.16071
df	167
Std Dev	0.61255

t Test

Test Statistic	0.0151
Prob > |t|	0.9880
Prob > t	0.4940
Prob < t	0.5060

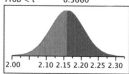

Confidence Intervals

Parameter	Estimate	Lower CI	Upper CI	1–Alpha
Mean	2.160714	2.067412	2.254016	0.950
Std Dev	0.612547	0.553306	0.686106	

Distributor Perception of Foreign Quality Greater Than or Equal to Domestic

Distributions

Q24 Foreign Quality >= domestic

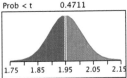

Moments

Mean	1.9457831
Std Dev	0.7487851
Std Err Mean	0.058117
upper 95% Mean	2.060532
lower 95% Mean	1.8310343
N	166

Test Mean=value

Hypothesized Value	1.95
Actual Estimate	1.94578
df	165
Std Dev	0.74879

t Test

Test Statistic	-0.0726
Prob > |t|	0.9422
Prob > t	0.5289
Prob < t	0.4711

1.75   1.85   1.95   2.05   2.15

Confidence Intervals

Parameter	Estimate	Lower CI	Upper CI	1–Alpha
Mean	1.945783	1.831034	2.060532	0.950
Std Dev	0.748785	0.675974	0.839313	

Distributor Perception That Domestic Brands are Losing Channel Power

Distributions

Q29 Domestic Brands Lose Channel Power

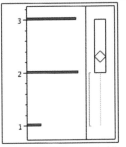

Quantiles

100.0%	maximum	3.0000
99.5%		3.0000
97.5%		3.0000
90.0%		3.0000
75.0%	quartile	3.0000
50.0%	median	2.0000
25.0%	quartile	2.0000
10.0%		1.0000
2.5%		1.0000
0.5%		1.0000
0.0%	minimum	1.0000

Moments

Mean	2.3035714
Std Dev	0.6813067
Std Err Mean	0.052564
upper 95% Mean	2.4073469
lower 95% Mean	2.1997959
N	168

Test Mean=value

Hypothesized Value	2.3
Actual Estimate	2.30357
df	167
Std Dev	0.68131

t Test

Test Statistic	0.0679
Prob > |t|	0.9459
Prob > t	0.4730
Prob < t	0.5270

2.10   2.20   2.30   2.40   2.50

Confidence Intervals

Parameter	Estimate	Lower CI	Upper CI	1–Alpha
Mean	2.303571	2.199796	2.407347	0.950
Std Dev	0.681307	0.615416	0.763123	